MAKE MONEY

with

FLIPPERS, FIXERS,

AND

RENOVATIONS

MAKE MONEY

with

FLIPPERS, FIXERS, AND RENOVATIONS

SECOND EDITION

GARY W. ELDRED, PhD

WILEY

John Wiley & Sons, Inc.

Copyright © 2008 by Gary W. Eldred, PhD. All rights reserved.

Published by John Wiley & Sons, Inc., Hoboken, New Jersey.
Published simultaneously in Canada.

For general information on our other products and services or for technical support, please contact our Customer Care Department within the United States at (800) 762-2974, outside the United States at (317) 572-3993 or fax (317) 572-4002.

Wiley also publishes its books in a variety of electronic formats. Some content that appears in print may not be available in electronic books. For more information about Wiley products, visit our web site at www.wiley.com.

Library of Congress Cataloging-in-Publication Data:

Eldred, Gary W.
 Make money with flippers, fixers, and renovations / Gary W. Eldred. — 2nd ed.
  p. cm.
 Includes index.
 ISBN 978-0-470-18344-1
  1. Real estate investment—United States.   I. Title.
 HD259.E38 2008
 332.63'243—dc22

                                                    2007045703

Printed in the United States of America.

10 9 8 7 6 5 4 3 2 1

CONTENTS

ACKNOWLEDGMENTS

I would like to acknowledge several people who have contributed to my work and this book. First, I thank His Highness Sheikh Dr. Sultan Bin Mohammed Al Qassimi, Supreme Council Member, UAE, Ruler of Sharjah, and Founder and President of American University of Sharjah. Due to his generosity, leadership, and vision, in less than a decade the American University of Sharjah has emerged as the leading university in the Middle East.

My thanks, too, go to Dr. R. Malcolm Richards, Dean of the School of Business and Management, for inviting me to AUS to develop a curriculum in real estate and for providing a first-class working environment within what has become one of the world's most dynamic and fastest growing property markets. In addition, my student assistants at AUS, Mohsen Mofid and Sadaf A. Fasihnia, deserve recognition for their valued help, without which I could not have made my publisher's deadlines. For her long-term help (20 manuscripts) and continued assistance, I owe a deep debt of appreciation to Barbara Smerage of Santa Fe, New Mexico.

Gary W. Eldred, Ph.D.

Flip, Fix, Renovate, Convert: Quick Paths to Profits

Would you like to double or triple your money in 12 months or less? Would you like to build quick profits of $10,000, $20,000, $100,000, or more—even though you lack cash or strong credit? Do you want to learn a moneymaking skill that you can put to work anywhere in North America (or, for that matter, almost anywhere in the world)? Would you prefer to work (full- or part-time) without set hours and without a boss looking over your shoulder? Would you like to achieve mid- to long-term financial freedom and personal independence?

If you answer "yes" to any of these questions, I've written this book for you.

In this book, you will learn how to earn big profits as you *entrepreneurially* create value for the buyers and tenants of your properties.

> **To maximize profits, entrepreneurs strategically improve their fixers.**

As a real estate entrepreneur, you will easily discover properties that you can buy for less than the profit potential they offer. But you won't just slap on a fresh coat of paint, lay down new carpet, and wash the windows. You will *strategically* improve the property to favorably distinguish it from competing properties. You will shape its features toward a select and profitable target of buyers, tenants, or investors. You work with your mind, not necessarily your hands.

Buying Right, Fixing, and Flipping Yield Great Profits in Any Market

In many cities today, high prices, low cash flows, and sluggish sales *seem to* signal the end of real estate opportunity. The media certainly promotes this dismal view. But, in fact, real estate pros laugh about the biased, no-nothing reporting of most journalists who write and broadcast articles on real estate—especially those silly scribes who write for the national personal finance magazines.[1]

And we pay no attention to media pundits (economists, financial planners, and others erroneously referred to as experts) who eagerly voice opinions just to get themselves in the news.

In periods of growth, we love our rapid buildup of equity (but strong buyer competition for properties—especially from amateurs who overpay—make good deals tougher to find). In cooler times, good deals multiply. As rapid market appreciation recedes until another day, as the greater fool momentum takes a vacation, we pros love the now open playing field where we can execute our entrepreneurial skills to create value.

In all times, properties offer promise for profitable improvement. But the most frequently recommended fix-up approach fails to adequately tap your imagination, intellect, and creativity. Indeed, the traditional fix-up approach almost encourages you to stifle yourself. "Appeal to the largest possible audience," authors advise. "Keep everything neutral. Don't offend anyone. Don't venture into the unknown. Sure, you might throw in a few *gee-whiz* features like a skylight or hot tub, but for the most part, just focus on clean and fresh."

Although such an approach can earn profits, it tosses out an entrepreneurial vision. It doesn't maximize profits. This common approach only steers you to rundown houses that you can buy at a steep discount. If no repairs are necessary, no deal. No bargain price, no deal. Consequently, when you adopt this bland, routine approach, you pass by many properties that could yield great returns.

---

[1]See, for example, one of the most foolish articles of this breed, "Stocks vs. Real Estate," *Money*, April 2007.

The Entrepreneurial Approach

Most beginning investors who fix and flip follow the traditional approach: Find a motivated seller who owns a property that looks bad and smells bad. Negotiate a bargain (below-market) price. Make cosmetic improvements. Resell at a profit.

If you follow this traditional approach to flipping, you will make money. But you won't make as much as you could. The deals you do will leave money on the table. Many deals you pass up—often because negotiations fail to give you a below-market price—sometimes overflow with possibilities that you have not learned to envision.

In contrast, adopt the entrepreneurial approach and you will capture profits the "look bad, smell bad, below-market price" approach misses. What is the entrepreneurial approach? Here's a description from Suzanne Brangham, author of *Housewise* (HarperCollins, 1987):

> As you compare neighborhoods and properties, keep your eye out for ideas you can use to improve the houses and apartment buildings you evaluate. Although most books and articles on real estate investing tell you to buy fixer-uppers, keep in mind that a fixer-upper is *any* property that you can redecorate, redesign, remodel, rezone, expand, improve, or romance. The name of the game is profitable creativity. You can make nearly any home or apartment [or neighborhood] live better, look better, and feel better. To profit from renovation, the properties you buy need not look like they've been mistreated and neglected for the past 20 years.

> **Entrepreneurs can create value with "perfect" properties.**

Throw out the idea that only rundown properties define a "fixer-upper." Sure, poorly maintained properties offer good potential for value-enhancing improvements. But to keen observers, even meticulously kept properties aren't immune to profitable change. When you stay alert to opportunity, you can make any property more desirable to potential buyers or tenants. Consider the experience of Raymond and Annie Brown.

The Browns Create Value in a Down Market

When Raymond Brown and his wife, Annie, bought a vacation retreat home they call Woodpecker Haven, Raymond says, "I thought it was a done property. It was only five years old."

Annie, though, thought about property from a value-creating perspective. As an interior designer with a forward-looking imagination, Annie simply remarked that the house "had great potential." As Raymond tells the story, "Here are some of the improvements my enterprising wife accomplished to transform a livable property into an exquisite home:

- Landscaped the front and rear yards
- Installed a drip irrigation system
- Built a stone fence around the pool
- Added decks around the rear of the house
- Installed in both bedrooms French doors that led out to the decks
- Remodeled the guest bedroom and bath to create a master bedroom for visitors
- Built in a fireplace, bookshelves, cabinets, and track lighting in the living room
- Trimmed trees and shrubs to enhance a picture-perfect view from the front porch"

Although Raymond and Annie invested $75,000 in these and other improvements, they added $175,000 in value—throughout a falling market. "We bought our Sonoma retreat," says Raymond, "just as property prices were peaking, and sold several years later, two months before prices bottomed out. . . . Yet we made a $100,000 profit. Our secret? Woodpecker Haven was a fixer-upper we renovated inside and out."

> **Build wealth in a falling market.**

> **If it can look better, live better, or generate more pizzazz, it's a "fixer."**

The Browns prove that a fixer is any property that could look better, live better, and feel better than it does. (Remember, at the time they bought the property, Woodpecker Haven was only five years old. Recall, too, the Browns made their big gains in a *falling* market.) To fix up a property (or neighborhood) may require you to scrape encrusted bubble gum off floors and counters, patch holes in the roof, fight a gnarled mass of weeds and debris in the backyard, pull out and replace rusted and obsolete kitchen and bathroom plumbing fixtures, or lobby city hall for cleaner streets, more services, and improved schools. But fixing up a property also can mean visualizing ways to redecorate, redesign, remodel, expand, or bring romance to the property.

My Awakening

Like most property owners and renovators, I originally adopted the boring fix-it approach to buying and improving my rental properties. Then, when I was enrolled in my doctoral program at the University of Illinois, I chanced upon a talk about real estate with one of my professors. He told me that after building a new house he (unsuccessfully) tried to sell his previous home. A year on the market, the house remained unsold, so the professor placed a tenant in the property. He asked if I would be interested in buying the house. I agreed to take a look.

Great House, No Appeal The house was located in a desirable neighborhood only a short bike ride from campus. As to physical condition, the house showed no disrepair. No buyer would have called this house a fixer. Yet, when I thought about making the house my home, I backed away. The house lacked warmth and cheer. It was dark inside. The color schemes made army olive look bright. Heavy custom-made drapes in the living room and bedrooms (of which my professor was especially proud) also added to the home's dreary feel.

> **Earn a 5:1 payback for imaginative improvements.**

"Thanks, but no thanks," I told my prof. Then, fortunately, a more creative friend visited the house with me and immediately began to visualize the changes that she would make to the house if she were to live there. With relatively minor changes, she could transform the property's look, feel, and livability. She proved to be right.

I did buy the property, made the suggested changes, and quickly resold the house at a price higher than my professor had been asking. My payback on out-of-pocket expenses was about five to one.

> **Create a *My Fair Lady* makeover.**

A Home, Not a House From that moment, I changed my perspective on fixers. I realized that to most profitably improve a house (or apartment unit) you must first think of it as a *home*. Then, abandon the mere fix-up mentality in favor of transformation. Don't merely dress up the property in a new outfit. Think of your work as Henry Higgins thought of his Cockney drudge in the movie *My Fair Lady*. Indeed, the profitable technique of "home staging" puts this principle into practice. Home stagers transform utilitarian houses into "fair ladies."

Unlimited Potential

To envision improvements, recognize that profitable properties come in all sizes, shapes, and types. Yes, judge a property for its fix-up potential but also envision more creative improvement. Do likewise for the neighborhood.

> **You can improve "perfect condition" properties in a dozen or more ways.**

Most importantly, evaluate potential improvements through the lens of market strategy. Create that combination of features and amenities for which targeted buyers (or tenants) will gladly pay a premium. Through market study, discover profitable ways to differentiate your properties from those of your competitors (other sellers or owners of for-sale and for-rent properties). Throughout this

Features which stand out. Can be seen

book you will learn to ask and answer many detailed questions that will help you exploit opportunities that a majority of investors and homebuyers miss. For starters, answer these questions:

1. *Livability.* How can you improve the floor plan, traffic patterns, resident privacy, egress, and ingress?

2. *Living space.* Can you add living space through a room addition or conversion (garage, porch, basement, attic)?

3. *Storage.* Where are the dead spaces that you could enhance for storage? What ideas can you borrow from the California Closet Company to add storage capacity without necessarily adding new storage space?

4. *Income potential.* How might you create independent living space such as an in-law suite or accessory apartment? Can you create private living space for a teenager or live-in help?

5. *Roommate living.* If you plan to hold (or sell) the property as a rental, how might you modify the space or living areas to more pleasantly accommodate roommates or other types of shared living arrangements?

6. *Rightsizing.* Are some rooms or areas too large or too small? Do the room count and functions (bedrooms, bathrooms, great room) best match the needs and wants of your most profitable target market? What changes are possible?

7. *Operating and maintenance costs.* Can you switch from high-maintenance materials to low- or no-maintenance items? What can you do to reduce the utility bills?

8. *Capital costs.* How can you minimize property taxes, property insurance, assessments, or mortgage interest for your buyers (or yourself)?

9. *Aesthetics.* How can you romance the property, add pizzazz, or enhance a bright, cheery, or warm feeling? *Landscaping*

10. *Views.* Can you enhance or create a pleasant view? (No, you don't need mountains or lakes. A flower garden or ivy-covered trellis can also provide a pleasing respite.) Can you eliminate any ugly or distasteful view? Can you add or relocate windows?

Near public spaces.

11. *Landscaping, trees, shrubs.* What can you add? What should you cut? Can you improve the yard's appearance with fertilizer, mulch, walkways, fountains, fish ponds, or fencing? Would a different type of grass grow better or look better?

12. *Security.* In our crime-conscious world, what can you do to diminish the home's susceptibility to break-ins?

13. *Safety.* Can you enhance the safety of the home for children, seniors, or just plain everyday living?

14. *Special-purpose use.* Can the property (or any part thereof) be profitably adapted for use as an office, artist's studio, or rentable storage area? Can you profitably adapt the property to better serve the needs of the disabled?

15. *Site.* Can you rightsize the site by acquiring part or all of a contiguous property or by subdividing or splitting off part of the existing lot? Does the size of the site allow for additional building, storage, or parking?

16. *Neighborhood.* What can you and neighborhood property owners do to upgrade or revitalize the community or neighborhood? Contrary to popular perception, you *can* change the location of a property. You can change the location when you improve the schools, redirect flow-through traffic, beautify properties, or reduce crime.

17. *Neighbors.* Sometimes a thoughtless or hostile neighbor can create value-diminishing problems for nearby property owners. What can you and other property owners do to bring that wayward neighbor into line?

18. *Legal.* What laws and regulations (zoning, building codes, homeowners association rules, easements, deed restrictions, environmental standards, health and safety ordinances) control what you can and cannot do with your property? When you learn the detailed ins and outs of these do's and don'ts, you avoid costly blunders and capitalize on seldom-noticed (or recently emerging) opportunities.

Obtain a change in zoning, a variance, or a special-use exception. You add value to a property. Use zoning codes and ordinances to discipline those scalawag property owners (tenants) whose behavior adversely affects neighborhood property values.

From these 18 possibilities, entrepreneurs create value for their properties. They systematically examine the house, garage, outbuildings, site, neighborhood, neighbors, and all laws, rules, and restrictions that regulate property use and design. Most buyers (and sellers) remain uninformed about many of these potential areas for profitable change. They typically inspect only for needed repairs and cosmetic improvements. They miss some of their best opportunities to enhance their returns.

> **Profit from the ignorance and oversight of others.**

Fortunately, such oversight works to your advantage: First, you face less competition for good properties. Second, due to the fact that sellers often fail to recognize the potential of their properties, you can buy great properties for much less than they are worth. In this sense, I don't necessarily mean far less than a property's current as-is market value, but rather a market value price that still yields a large margin of profit.

Occasionally, you can find steeply discounted prices offered by those motivated sellers that most real estate authors write about. But to succeed as an entrepreneurial fixer, go beyond that limited approach. *Think entrepreneurially*. Multiply your opportunities for profit.

Multiple Ways to Profit

As you master the art of creating value, you can earn your gains and build your wealth in at least five ways.

Fix and Quick Flip

Use the fix-and-flip approach to buy, renovate, and sell a property within a short period. This technique works well to generate fast cash. You can then pyramid these profits to reinvest in larger and higher-profit projects. Suzanne Brangham (the author of *Housewise*) began her

> **Quickly build up your cash through fix and flip.**

fix-and-quick-flip career with an unseemly $40,000 condominium (that she sold six months later for $80,000). Then, over a period of years, Suzanne worked herself through dozens of properties all the way up to multimillion-dollar executive homes.

However, under current tax law, multiple quick flips expose you to income tax liabilities. You need to consult tax counsel to perhaps work these transactions within either a corporate structure, an LLC, or a tax-deferred retirement account such as an IRA or 401(k). Yet, for your first several deals, fix and quick flip can put cash in your bank account faster and more surely than any other legal moneymaking opportunity.

Find out about all of these

Fix and Flip Slowly (Two Years)

Although current law taxes the fix-and-quick-flip rehabber less than kindly, it treats the two-year owner-occupant far more favorably. If you

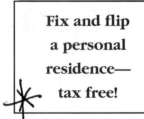

> **Fix and flip a personal residence— tax free!**

live in a property for at least two years, your gain of up to $250,000 ($500,000 for a married couple) will land in your bank account tax free! Use this technique five or six times over a period of 10 or 12 years and you could easily build up a nice-sized sum of $500,000 or more.[2]

Fix, Hold, Refinance

I generally prefer to fix and hold properties as rentals. This approach helps you pay no taxes on your gain and, after a year or so, you can pull tax-free cash out through a refinance. You can use that tax-free refi money as a down payment to acquire another property.

---

[2]For more on this trend, see "Tax Law Is Leading Some to Serial Homebuying," *New York Times*, March 30, 2003, B-8. The *New York Times* archives of past articles are now available online without charge.)

(handwritten marginalia at top of page:)

H+J. 65,000   140,000   75,000
Chu. 126,000 150,000   24,000
      191,000 290,000 $99,000 Equity · $99,000

> **Pull out tax-free cash with a refinance.**

For example, in one of my early deals, I paid $106,000 (appraised at $106,500) for a property and put $26,000 down. Then I creatively improved the property for about $15,000 in renovation costs. After these improvements, the property appraised at $150,000. I refinanced and pulled out $40,000 in cash. I placed that $40,000 as down payments on two other properties. Creating value with fixers not only earns short-term profits but accelerates your wealth building with leverage (borrowed money).

(Note that the profits in this example did not occur because I bought at a steeply discounted purchase price. I earned these profits because I knew how to recognize and realize the potential of the property, whereas the sellers did not.)

Fix, Hold, Flip (Trade) Up

(handwritten marginalia:) Trade up

Here's another way to pyramid real estate profits and avoid income taxes. Section 1031 of the Internal Revenue Code permits real estate investors to trade up tax free.

> **Use a Section 1031 exchange to pyramid your wealth and pay no taxes on your gains.**

You buy a $100,000 property and through profitable improvement boost its market value to $160,000. You want to invest the equity you've created into a more expensive property. Moreover, assume that a sale would net you a taxable gain of $40,000. Alas, the Internal Revenue Service would claim a chunk of that money. So instead of selling, you find a more expensive property you would like to own. You then execute a Section 1031 exchange. Your full $40,000 of gain (less trading fees) gets counted toward the purchase price of this more expensive acquisition. You pay the IRS nothing.

(handwritten marginalia:) Sec. 1031 exchange

Repeat the process until you reach your financial goals. You need never pay tax on your equity gains. Your wealth builds tax free. If along the way you need cash, don't sell. Draw tax-free cash against an equity line of credit. (Like all tax laws, various rules apply to this technique.

Consult a tax pro to evaluate the ways you can best execute such a ta-savings strategy.)

The Home (or Neighborhood) You Can't Afford

Although I've aimed this book at investors, homebuyers can put this knowledge to good use. With the run-up in home prices since the late 1990s, some of the most desirable homes and neighborhoods are now priced out of reach for many hopeful homebuyers. If that's a situation you face, apply the creative techniques discussed throughout the following pages. Buy a "fixer" and move into the home or neighborhood that you otherwise could not afford.

> **Buy a fixer to conquer the problem of affordability.**

Vanquish Your Fears: Become an Entrepreneurial Investor

Throughout my career I've talked with hundreds of people who have expressed an interest in buying and improving properties. They know that fixers yield better returns than other investments. Yet, few take the first step. Why? Because they block themselves with a multitude of fears. In reality, *none* of these fears are warranted. I know, because I've been there. Let me recount my own less-than-promising start:

1. *Zero experience.* My entire experience with property improvement had consisted of cutting grass at home to earn my high school allowance.
2. *Lack of cash and credit.* As a 21-year-old college student, I scraped together $1,000 and financed my first purchase with a seller-held land contract.
3. *No technical knowledge.* I did not know anything about electrical systems, carpentry, plumbing, painting, or wallpapering.

I soon found out that I lacked any ability to skillfully pursue these crafts. (Even today, after having profitably bought, managed, improved, and sold several score of properties, I wouldn't try to change a faucet washer or repair a broken window.)

4. *No time.* By age 26, I was carrying a full load of coursework in my doctoral program, teaching at two universities (one full-time, one part-time), and overseeing my portfolio of rental houses and apartments.

5. *Poor economy.* During the early years of my investing, the U.S. economy was in the pits—high unemployment, skyrocketing inflation, a country running out of resources (so we were told), and a supposedly bleak future as the land of the rising sun eclipsed our leadership in manufacturing.

> **Entrepreneurs build wealth. Most people build a pile of excuses.**

Do I tell the facts of my entry into real estate to trumpet accomplishments against tough circumstances? No; nearly every successful investor I know got started under similar conditions—not in the details, but in the sense that they, too, met head-on many constraints of time, money, credit, job, family, knowledge, and experience. Yet, they acted.

They did not build a wall of excuses. They moved forward because they understood that their rewards stood much greater than the potential risks.

Yes, You Need Skills

Investors who succeed vanquish their fears and move forward, but they do not careen recklessly or randomly. They nurture eight skills that distinguish winners from whiners:

1. Search to learn what they really need to know.
2. Delegate tasks and manage others who perform the needed work.
3. Discipline their use of money and time.

Design →

4. Open an inquisitive mind that persistently searches for new and better ideas.
5. Accept the challenge of work and productive activity.
6. Accept responsibility and review mistakes.
7. Commit to written personal and financial goals and write a plan for achievement.
8. Love real estate and a sense of accomplishment.

The first seven of these skills lead to success in nearly any field. But for personal and financial success in real estate—and especially in the field of real estate entrepreneurship—enjoy your work.

I love looking at properties, talking about real estate, discovering the latest trends, and all the while trying to figure out how to apply something I've learned to one or more of my properties.

> **Build wealth without "work."**

Each year, I travel the United States to look at properties and explore local markets. On my frequent trips to Europe, Asia, and the Middle East, I do the same. I also read new books that come out in the field and stay abreast of a dozen or more journals, magazines, newspapers, and newsletters.

Yet, none of these activities seem like "work" in the traditional sense of that word. Even though you may not choose such a high level of exploration and discovery, to the degree that you do, you multiply the types of properties where you spot profit potential.

My Promise

Unlike many books aimed at beginning investors, this book doesn't feed you pie in the sky. It doesn't send you into the market looking for deals

> **Real investors focus on realistic, doable deals.**

that occur no more than 1 out of every 50 times. It doesn't pretend to give you a canned, step-by-step approach as to exactly what types of properties, price ranges, and neighborhoods provide the most profitable opportunities. Nor does this book provide you phone scripts.

Authors who peddle such nonsense ought to have someone unplug their keyboard.

Why do these step-by-step, everything-you-need-to-know books fail? For at least eight reasons:

1. *Local markets differ*. What worked best in San Diego or Albuquerque last year may next year prove impossible. And it may never have worked in Peoria or Paducah.
2. *Relative prices change*. Like stocks, properties, neighborhoods, and price trends run from hot to lukewarm to cold. To profit most with the least risk, anticipate and monitor cycles.
3. *Target markets differ*. To earn high profits and create value, direct your market strategy toward a well-defined target market. Generic strategies miss the mark.
4. *Competition differs*. Develop your best strategy with full knowledge of competing properties, their features, and their price ranges.
5. *Financing differs*. Great financing can lift a so-so deal into the highly profitable category. Likewise, adverse terms of financing may kill an otherwise good opportunity.
6. *Improvement costs differ.* Costs vary among different locales and among different contractors for the same improvements at the same property.
7. *Originality pays big dividends*. Through vision and market research, discover creative possibilities that give your strategies the difference that sets up the distinguishing difference for your buyers (tenants).
8. *Ideas, not sweat equity*. The largest rewards go to people who think. You can't expect to achieve superior returns if you merely follow someone else's one-size-fits-all do's and don'ts.

The best-seller, *In Search of Excellence* (over five million copies sold), by Tom Peters and Bob Waterman (Harper & Row, 1982), presumed to prescribe the rules of success for corporate America. As evidence, Peters and Waterman showcased 20 (supposed) premier companies. Yet, two years after that book was published, *Business Week* ran a cover story entitled "Oops." It turned out that six of these so-called premier companies had hit the skids. The Peters and Waterman prescription no longer seemed to work.

How does this fact relate to real estate? It illustrates the basic point: To earn quick (or slow) profits in real estate, throw out the simplistic step-by-step instruction manuals. The rules of the game change. You simplistic can't create the future you want by thoughtlessly following the "six easy steps" that might have worked in the past.

> **Increase your profits. Tailor a strategy to your area.**

Instead, stack the odds for success in your favor. Learn to match your strategy to the market conditions that prevail at the time you invest. Craft a business plan to fulfill the most pressing (and profitable) needs of the day.

The foundation principle of marketing, "Find a need (want) and fill it," applies to flip-and-fix entrepreneurs just as it applies to Toyota and Nike. Your properties will generously reward you when you give your customers (buyers, tenants) the best value proposition they can find. That's the principle this book shows you how to put into practice—a principle that sharpens your entrepreneurial vision.

CHAPTER 2

Market Strategy Trumps Market Value

To naive investors, market value tells all they need to know to score a good deal. Buy for less than market value, that's great! Pay more, and you made a mistake. Compounding this error, naïve investors judge possibilities in terms of comparable properties. They let similar competitors dictate the benchmarks for their fix-ups, renovations, and pricing.

Naïve investors make money, but they miss far greater profits. If you adopt an entrepreneurial eye for opportunity, you pocket these extra profits. You look at market value as one data point—but only one. As Donald Trump rightly boasts, "We figure out ways to break through the comps on every one of our projects."

Think about it like this. If you own a share of IBM, that share is just like every other IBM share (of the same stock class). When you sell, market value rules. No one achieves a price higher than market value. Likewise, neither you nor anyone else need sell at a price less than market value. At any given time, that one share of IBM has one and only one price.

> **Entrepreneurs find those differences that make the *profitable* difference.**

No real estate entrepreneur would ever judge value in this narrow and passive way. Even though so-called comp properties share similar features, it is within the power of the entrepreneur to find or create different features that lift the appeal and the

17

price of a given property to a selected type of buyer (or tenant). The entrepreneur thinks of strategy, not merely repairs and fix-up. To clarify, look more closely into the definition of real estate market value. When you understand market value, you understand why you need to look beyond this narrow and misleading touchstone of value.

> **Learn to exploit the weaknesses of "market value."**

Market Value Defined

Real estate appraisers define *market value* to include the following presumptions:

1. *Most probable selling price. Most probable price* reflects that (contrary to common belief) market value does not assume one "correct" value for a property. Instead, market value presumes a range of values.

2. *Competitive open market.* Strictly speaking, the term *market value* presumes an active market (similar to shares of stocks) with numerous look-alike comparable properties up for sale (or rent). Ideally, the concept works best in cookie-cutter, tract home subdivisions. It works least for properties with unique features (advantages or disadvantages).

3. *Fair sale.* Market value presumes that buyers and sellers enjoy "walkaway" willpower. Neither party feels pressure to buy or sell because of time, money, or manipulative sales tactics. Have you ever attended a free dinner gathering where you sat face-to-face with a time-share salesman? The property prices obtained during these sales presentations greatly exceed market value. With limited exception, if you resell a time-share, you're lucky to pocket 60 to 70 percent of the price you paid.

4. *Equal knowledge.* Market value presumes that buyers and sellers know all of the advantages and disadvantages of a subject property as well as the prices and terms of sale for all nearby comparable properties that have sold recently.

5. *Terms of sale.* Market value presumes that the sellers do
   not offer desirable terms of financing or favorable concessions (e.g., sellers pay all closing costs, sellers carry back a
   low-interest-rate mortgage, sellers include valuable personal
   property).

Assuming these five conditions of sale, appraisers perform three
valuations: (1) the cost approach, (2) the income approach, and (3) the
comparable sales approach. Typically, residential appraisers emphasize
the comp sales approach. They use the cost and income approaches to
cross check their results.

The Comparable Sales Approach

> **Comp sales
> inform, but they
> don't dictate.**

The comp sales approach seems reasonable. To estimate the price at which a subject property will sell,
find out the recent sales prices of similar nearby
houses. (See Figure 2.1.)

Adjustment Process (Selected Features)			
	Comp 1	*Comp 2*	*Comp 3*
Sales price	$112,560	$106,720	$105,530
Features			
Sales concessions	0	−5,000	0
Financing concessions	−7,500	0	0
Date of Sale	0	+5,000	0
Location	0	0	−10,000
Floor plan	0	+2,500	0
Garage	+5,500	0	+8,500
Pool, patio, deck	−4,500	−6,500	0
Indicated value of subject	$106,060	$102,720	$104,030

Figure 2.1   The Comparable Sales Approach.

To perform an appraisal, an appraiser itemizes the features of the property to be appraised. Then he selects three look-alike properties (preferably from the same neighborhood). He notes the following information:

1. All property addresses.
2. Where each comp property is located relative to the subject properties.
3. The actual price at which each comp property was sold.
4. The source of information for the comp property data.
5. Any seller financing or concessions.
6. The dates on which each of the comp properties closed.
7. A basic feature-by-feature comparison of each comp property vis-à-vis the subject property. Where differences are found, the appraiser estimates the value of each difference. However, note that positive differences result in a negative adjustment (and vice versa). Why? Because if the subject property lacks a certain advantageous feature, it will typically sell at a lower price.
8. Adjust the sales price of each comparable property according to how it differs from the subject property.

To complete this last step, the appraiser asks, "What price would the buyers of this similar property have paid *if* the features of this house had precisely matched those of the subject property?"

The Market Value Conclusion

Once an appraiser completes this comparison and adjusts for property differences, the estimated market value of the subject property practically jumps out at you. If three similar nearby properties show adjusted sales prices that range between $240,200 and $260,050, it doesn't take Einstein intelligence to place a $250,000 market value on the subject property. All other things equal, that's the best-guess price for the property if its sale meets all of the conditions of a market value sale.

Strengths of the Appraisal Process

At its best, a market value appraisal serves two purposes: (1) It provides a common denominator for discussions about past and present property values; and (2) it offers a disinterested third party's informed opinion.

Common Denominator

People buy and sell real estate under all sorts of terms, conditions, negotiating pressures, and assumptions. To merely know that a property down the block sold for $378,000 is to know very little. Did the sellers offer carryback financing? Did they pay all closing costs? Did they sell-by-owner? Were they represented by a competent real estate agent? Likewise, we could ask questions about the buyers' pressures, motives, market knowledge, negotiating skills, and credit-worthiness. Any and all of these factors can and do affect selling prices. Therefore, to talk about price without knowledge can easily lead to error.

> **Market value provides a uniform standard for comparison.**

But, when we talk about "market value," the ability to communicate increases. Since conditions of sale are set by the definition itself, market value provides a standard or benchmark of value without which conversations about selling prices would lack clarity.

Disinterested Third Party

Buyers, sellers, the guy or gal down the street, the mailman, or the FedEx driver—all may express opinions about whether the price of a property seems too high, too low, or just about right. But where did they get their information? What do they really know about the property? What biases do they hold? Do self-interest or emotional attachment shade their judgment?

Should you place confidence in such opinions? Probably not. Still, when an appraiser *competently* estimates market value, you've an

> **Comp sales give you objective, market-based information.**

objective opinion that you can count on. Just as important, appraisers display the data on which they base their value estimates. You can judge for yourself whether they've got their facts straight and whether their interpretations and reasoning make sense.

Overall, these two strengths (common denominator, disinterested expertise) explain why most homebuyers, investors, sellers, and mortgage lenders use market value appraisals to inform their decision making.

Weaknesses of the Appraisal Process

Although you should use market value to inform your buy/sell decisions, never let it dictate your estimate of value. Even a competently prepared appraisal does not answer the strategic (entrepreneurial) questions that you need to address. Here's why.

Rearview Mirror

Even when correct, market value appraisals work as a rearview mirror. They reveal what's behind you. They do not illuminate the future. An appraiser looks only to *past* sales prices. Data in the appraisal report fail to explain how the market may evolve over the coming 3, 6, or 12 months (or longer).

> **Comp sales never (purposely) alert you to strategic improvements.**

Indeed, the comp sales included in an appraisal report often look even further backward than the appraisal report indicates. That's because appraisals cite the date a sale closed, not the date the buyers and sellers actually struck their deal. In some cases, buyers and sellers may have signed their sales contract two to four months prior to the date that settlement eventually occurred.

You Need Data about the Future   To profitably flip or fix a property within, say, a 3- to 24-month time frame, carefully forecast what the market may throw at you in the months to come. Never assume that the supply-and-demand situation that prevailed three to six months ago will continue unchanged.

What if you arrange short-term financing that falls due and you count on a sale to generate the necessary cash? Or maybe you want to refinance out of a high-cost acquisition and improvement loan into lower-cost, long-term financing? Either way, appraise the future, not the past. The headlines about foreclosure and "payment shock" reveal the problems that surface when people fail to guard against changes in both property and mortgage markets.

Buy, Fix, and Hold   Even when you hold a property as a rental, plan for potential shifts in the short term. Will the property rent up quickly at a premium rent? Or will you face hot-and-heavy competition from several new apartment or condo complexes that are scheduled to come to market shortly?

As a buy-fix-hold investor, also assess the long-term potential for development. Ideally, buy properties in those areas where shortages of buildable land, high construction costs, or government zoning and environmental restrictions minimize competition from new subdivision, apartment, and condo projects (if you're working with residential properties).

Narrow Focus

Savvy investors compare potential appreciation rates among neighborhoods, communities, and types of properties. But a market value appraisal gives merely a glimpse of the pricing for one type of property in one area of a single city.

To illustrate, assume that you can buy and hold for at least five years one of two properties:

1. You can buy property A at a price $10,000 below its market value, or

2. You can buy property B at a price $10,000 above its market value.

Property A will probably appreciate 2 percent per year over the next five years. Property B will likely appreciate 6 percent per year over the next five years. Your purchase price for either property equals $150,000. Which do you choose?

Nearly all popular books on real estate urge you to search for properties that you can buy for less than market value. Basically, a sound idea. But what if you hold for perhaps 2, 5, 10 years or longer? With an extended time frame, forecast appreciation potential. It often turns out that bargain-priced properties show up more frequently in neighborhoods where values show slow (or no) rates of appreciation.

Bargain Price or Appreciation Potential?   Here's the answer to the above question: Property B gives you the most profit. Assuming a current market value for the property of $140,000 (remember, you paid $10,000 above market) and a 6 percent yearly rate of appreciation, after five years property B is worth $188,720, whereas A would show a market value of just $176,800. After 10 years, property B's value would shoot up to $254,395, whereas property A's value would have edged up to just $195,364.

> **Go mainly for appreciation potential, not necessarily a bargain price.**

Smart investors love to buy properties at below-market prices. But before you jump to snag a presumably good deal, compare relative values across areas and property types. Smart investors know that over the mid to long run, strong appreciation will outweigh today's immediate discount. Warren Buffett says that he would rather buy a company with great potential at a fair price than buy a mediocre company at a bargain price. Look at the past and present, but your decisions should chiefly envision the future. Different properties will experience much different futures.

Condo or House?   To illustrate through personal example: In the early 1980s, I was buying properties in Dallas, Texas. Similar to the early to mid-2000s, condominiums were all the rage. Homebuyers and investors were buying them almost as fast as they came to market. Yet, I thought, *something's crazy here.*

> **Always compare the prices of competing *types* of properties.**

Within the same neighborhood, condos were then selling at $100 per square foot, while perfectly nice single-family houses were selling at $65 per square foot. It seemed obvious that relative to condos, houses provided a far better buy. So going against the trend of the day, I bought houses. Within a few years, condomania subsided. Homebuyers and investors came to realize what I had figured out several years earlier. As a result, their buying shifted from condos to houses. Condo prices suffered. House prices shot up. Even if I had originally bought a new condo at a price 10 percent below market, the houses I bought at market value would still have proved the more profitable investment.

The Appraisal Process Shuns Entrepreneurial Vision

As an entrepreneurial fix-up investor, discover those properties (or locations) that offer (or could offer) unique features that a select target market of buyers (renters) would value highly. The

> **Very few appraisers build wealth in real estate.**

appraisal process provides clues toward this goal only by chance, not design. Appraisers rely only on comp properties whose existing features closely match those of a subject property. Their appraisals of market value never point out those location, site, or building features that could significantly boost a property's value. To a slight degree, price adjustments for feature differences may provide a glimpse of insight, but typically they do not.

Broaden your perspective. When you survey the sales prices (or rent levels) of competitive properties, look for those striking and unique differences that really give some properties a distinct competitive edge. Appraisers follow the appraisal process. They hate property differences and love similarities. As an entrepreneur, view the market from a contrasting perspective. Find or create those differences that really make a startling, advantageous difference to your buyers and tenants.

Summing Up the Appraisal Process

Most homebuyers and property investors naively focus on market value. They view properties only to learn current market prices. Then they use this market information to benchmark their purchase offers. The bigger their price discount from market value, the better their buy.

Entrepreneurs choose a somewhat different strategy. Yes, they, too, try to buy at a below-market price. But that's not their prime goal. Instead, they evaluate the market to achieve three more objectives: (1) Entrepreneurs forecast the quantity and quality of direct competition that may be coming to market; (2) they compare types of properties, neighborhoods, cities, and countries to discover properties and locations that offer the best *relative* values and potential for appreciation; and (3) they look at properties to figure the amount of value they can create.

Talk with successful investors. You will find that few have earned their fortunes by picking up properties at prices 30 percent below their current market value. From time to time, all of us do score such bargains. But over a career, to build wealth, we most want to gain appreciation, create value, and, for rentals, generate positive cash flows.

You Need More Market Data

To achieve rehab and investment profits, follow the appraisal process and research past sales prices of properties whose features and locations closely match the properties that you may buy. To understand and forecast a changing competitive environment, you need more facts about the area's trends. You boost profits and minimize risks when you rely on detailed supply and demand data to discover and create a profitable strategy:

> **Eagles fly higher than vultures.**

1. *New construction.* Check with the local government planning and zoning offices. Find out the number of subdivision, apartment, and condo projects that are planned or are under construction. Where are the new projects located? What price (rent) ranges prevail? What features do they include? (Also, determine new office, retail, and industrial projects. These projects may help create additional residential demand. Of course, if you're investing commercial, view such projects as potential competitors—as well as potential demand; e.g., new retail may spark demand for office space and vice versa.)

2. *Buildable land.* Does the geographical area you're looking at include large tracts of nearby vacant land? Or do land shortages set the norm? How difficult is it for builders and developers to get their land development and building permits approved?

3. *Inventory of homes for sale.* Realtors track this number weekly. Is it trending up or down? At the current rate of sales, how many months of inventory remain? Is this number shrinking or lengthening? Ask a Realtor to break the figures down by price range, location, and type of property.

4. *Time on market.* On average, listed properties may sell in a matter of weeks, or sales may take six months or more. Where is your market trending?

5. *Sales price/asking price.* In hot markets, properties may sell for more than their asking prices. In slow markets, sellers may eventually come down from their list prices by 10 percent to 20 percent or more. Where does your market stand?

6. *Vacancy rates.* Does the area show an increasing or decreasing trend in vacancies? Check houses, apartments, rental condo units, and commercial/industrial space. What areas show the most (least) strength?

7. *Rental rates.* Are rents increasing or decreasing? Are the large apartment complexes offering rent concessions such as a free bicycle, no security deposit, or short-term leases? Monitor vacancies and rental rates according to property features, pricing categories, and locations.

8. *Mortgage delinquencies and foreclosures.* When mortgage delinquencies and foreclosures increase, bargain prices become more plentiful. But also, a growing number of mortgage defaults signals market softness.

9. *Types of buyers (renters).* What types of buyers (renters) do you plan to appeal to? What features and amenities do they value highly? What differences can you create for your properties that will make the big and deciding differences to your customers?

10. *Pricing and financing.* What price and/or terms can you offer that will generate a good profit and a great buy for your market?

Want to maximize your returns? Obtain detailed knowledge of the features and sales prices of comp properties, a good forecast of competitive trends, and a deep feeling for the likes, dislikes, turn-ons, and turnoffs of targeted buyers (tenants). With this advantage, you position yourself to develop a winning investment strategy. With one eye on competitors and one eye on your potential customers, craft your improvement strategy to create a preferred value proposition (PVP).

Before people choose a place to live, shop, or work, they typically compare competing properties—often in different neighborhoods.

> **Build a competitive advantage for your properties.**

They weigh features, location, price, and terms. Then they go for the best value they can find that meets or surpasses their wants, needs, and expectations. Incorporate this fact into your value-creating efforts. Ask, "How can I best make my property stand above its competitors in the eyes of buyers (renters), yet do so in a way that gives me a wide margin of profit?"

CHAPTER 3

Your Formula for Creating Value

What distinguishes professional, astute entrepreneurs from the many amateurs who "fix and flip"? Amateurs buy a property, fix it up, and then price it high enough to recoup their expenses plus, say, another $10,000, $20,000, or $100,000 in profit. Amateurs use a cost-plus-profit figure to arrive at their (hoped for) selling price. Bad idea. This naive way of pricing explains why many investors lose money on their fix-up work. With cost-plus pricing, their asking prices frequently exceed market reality.

> **Calculate how much buyers will pay before you budget the cost of purchase and fixing.**

Professionals first study the market. They inspect competing properties. They evaluate the features, strengths, and weaknesses of these properties. They track asking prices, sales prices, and rent levels. Professionals contrast and compare how a property looks today with how it might look tomorrow. Even more, they imagine a target market of buyers (renters) to whom they plan to appeal. Professionals learn everything about their potential customers. After they think through facts, visions, and forecasts, professionals design their improvement strategy and calculate their potential profits according to the profit formula shown in Figure 3.1.

Minimum improved value (MIV)	$ _____
Less	
Purchase price	_____
Acquisition costs	_____
Improvement costs	_____
Financing costs	_____
Other holding costs	_____
Selling costs	_____
Opportunity costs	_____
Oops factor	_____
Income taxes	_____
Net profit	$ _____

Figure 3.1   Your Formula for Profits.

The Pieces of the Puzzle

Think of the profit formula in Figure 3.1 as a jigsaw puzzle. Each entry forms a piece of the puzzle. To succeed, put the figures together in a way that reveals profits.

> **Arrange the pieces until you see a picture of profits.**

In reality, the pieces of the puzzle vary in size. Through your skill, knowledge, negotiating, and creative efforts, the entrepreneurial investor works through a series of iterations—or we might call them *what-if* calculations.

When the fixer costs or purchase price, for example, seem too high, the entrepreneur looks for ways to whittle them down. Or maybe the estimated improved value seems too low to make the project come out right. In that case, take another look at your renovation plan. Figure more or better ways to create value than you've currently come up with. This and the remaining chapters provide scores of ideas that explore every piece of your profit

20 - 30,000 profit per
25 ung.
le lieuse ye.
& 150,000

formula. You join together the pieces that yield a boost to your bank balance.

Minimum Improved Value (MIV)

Stephen Covey advises, "Begin with the end in mind." So, your profit formula begins with this question: What's the lowest reasonable price at which I know I could sell this property once I've completed the changes that I envision for the property and/or its neighborhood? To determine this end point of your fixer efforts, combine your knowledge of market prices (the appraisal process) with your insights about how to create a competitive advantage for the property.

> **Keep your MIV well within the price range of the neighborhood.**

Except in unusual circumstances, limit the minimum improved values (MIVs) of your properties to no more than 80 percent of the top selling prices in the neighborhood. If you aim higher, you may overshoot the market. Properties that push the high end of a neighborhood price range typically prove themselves more difficult to sell. (But skill and effective promotion do create exceptions to this general rule.) Nevertheless, well-designed properties priced in the low- to mid-price range of a neighborhood tend to sell quickly. When you acquire at the low end, you gain more upside potential. You achieve more without exceeding apparent price limits.

80% of Neigh. Values

Purchase Price

As mentioned, most fix-it, flip-it books say that to make a deal work, buy your fix-up property at a price 25 percent to 30 percent below its as-is market value. Not true. Entrepreneurial renovators do not just fix up or repair properties. They find hidden values. They create value. They turn sows' ears into silk purses. They revitalize neighborhoods. They forecast area appreciation. When

> **Discover hidden value.**

buying off-plan, they figure which projects are best positioned to experience price increases.

I remind you of these points for two reasons: (1) Those investors
who seek 30 percent discounts often pass up properties that offer far
higher profit potential—even when the sellers won't discount their
property that much. When you evaluate a property,
calculate total profit potential. A steep discount
helps achieve that end—but it's not necessary.
(2) When you require an outsized (and often un-
realistic) price discount, you spend valuable time-
chasing deals that are tough to find.

Don't get me wrong. Negotiate steep discounts and bargain prices whenever possible.
And Chapter 10 shows you where and how to increase your odds of doing so. But never confuse
the profits earned from purchase discounts with
those earned through value-creating improve-
ments. If you miss the difference, you will invest time and money on
renovations when you might just as well flip the property and pocket
some quick, easy profits.

> **Negotiate bargain prices, but don't limit yourself to steeply discounted properties.**

Acquisition Costs

In addition to acquisition cost, you pay for title insurance, property
inspections, attorney fees, appraisal, survey, mortgage fees, and other
closing expenses. You can reduce these costs through negotiation and
comparative shopping. But there's no way to eliminate them. Include a
realistic figure to cover these costs.

Improvement Costs

Your improvement costs may include amounts for labor, materials,
landscaping, design fees, and government permits. When reviewing
cost estimates from contractors, itemize these figures into detailed

create value.

> **Reduce the costs of your improvements as you also enhance their appeal.**

categories. Then attack each one. Search for the most cost-effective means to solve each repair problem or to capitalize on each opportunity to create value. Never accept the first cost estimate you receive. Never accept a contractor's *gross* bid for a job. Review each line item. Savvy cost management can sometimes turn so-so deals into real moneymakers. (We cover tips on working with contractors later in this chapter.)

Financing Costs

During the period you hold a property, pay interest on any amounts you have borrowed to acquire the property or to fund the costs of improvements. In addition, you may have to pay points, a loan origination fee, and a mortgage application fee. If you raise funds from a partner to help finance your acquisition and improvements, the amount you pay for these monies also counts as a cost of financing.

As with all other costs, planning slashes the costs. Chapter 12 shows how to achieve this result by using short-term mortgage assumptions, lease options, "subject to" purchases, and similar techniques of creative finance. We'll also discuss the FHA 203(k) mortgage, which permits owner-occupant homebuyers to roll nearly all of their costs of purchase, acquisition, closing, and improvement into one mortgage. What's even better, your subsequent buyer can assume this mortgage for only a small fee.

Other Holding Costs

Even if you hold a property for just three to six months before you resell it, you'll pay property and liability insurance premiums, property taxes, and utility bills. These amounts add more costs to charge against your potential profits.

Selling Costs

Most investors use real estate agents to sell their properties. Normally, agents charge 4 to 7 percent of a property's sales price. However, if you follow the marketing pointers provided in Chapter 9, you eliminate the Realtor's commission. You pay for advertising, promotion, and perhaps bird-dog fees, and you may pay some settlement expenses for your buyer.

> **Learn how to profitably sell by owner.**

Opportunity Costs

To buy, flip, and/or renovate, plan a strategy, look for deals, negotiate, supervise contractors, and sell the property. These activities require time and effort. Even though such efforts don't draw down your cash, still figure them into your profit formula.

> **Pay yourself for labor you perform.**

How much do you think your time is worth? Given your job skills and education, how much could you earn per hour working in your own field? The more you earn, the more it will pay you to hire other people to perform as much of your work as possible. More importantly, never count as part of your fix-up profits any hands-on renovation work that you perform. If you actually paint, hammer, plumb, cut grass, or finish floors, sum up the value of this labor as an opportunity cost. Don't confuse "wages" you earn for work with those profits you earn through entrepreneurship and strategy. Build wealth through real estate, not as a self-employed carpenter or painter.

Oops Factor

Unfortunately, planning does not always lead to perfect results. We make mistakes. The people we hire make mistakes. Ballpark estimates grow into cost overruns. A three-month fix and flip stretches into a five- or six-month project. Interest rates shoot up and shut your target buyers out of the market. Your MIV becomes a maximum. When any or all of these setbacks occur, the *oops* factor allows you a margin of safety.

How much should you allocate to the *oops* factor? It depends. For simple jobs in hot markets, 1 or 2 percent of your property's MIV will prove adequate. For larger or more complex projects, use 5 to 10 percent of MIV.

Another approach to the *oops* factor is to identify cost estimates that present the most uncertainty. Then, figure bottom-line profits under two assumptions: (1) low-end costs; (2) high-end costs. When the deal still looks good with the high-end cost estimates, go for it. If not, rethink your strategy. Search out ideas and bids from other contractors. If no solution appears, shift to another possibility.

> **Oops! We all make mistakes. Budget for them.**

Income Taxes

If you plan to fix and flip, as opposed to fix and hold, discuss your sales strategy with a tax advisor. Typically, if you sell within 12 months after you've purchased a property, the IRS taxes your gain at ordinary income tax rates. (For most investors, ordinary tax rates range between 25 and 40 percent.) Even worse, should you fix and flip three or four properties within, say, a two-year time frame, the IRS may call you a *dealer*.

> **Don't let the IRS call you a dealer.**

Name-Calling Can Hurt You   As a child you may have recited, "Sticks and stones may break my bones, but names will never hurt me." Well, if the IRS calls you a dealer, it will hurt you. You may lose all right to claim long-term capital gains from real estate on your income tax return. The IRS may classify every property you own (except your home) as inventory. And when you sell inventory, you cannot enjoy those relatively low capital gain rates that run just 10 to 20 percent of your gain. (You might escape this issue by using various LLCs to separate your property hold-ings. Ask a tax/legal pro.)

The IRA Tax-Deferred Option   Personal finance magazines men-tion the fact that you may be able to buy real estate through a self-directed IRA or employer-sponsored, tax-deferred retirement plans such as the 401(k), Keogh, or SEP. You will need to use a third-party retirement plan administrator to handle your transactions. Nevertheless, you call the shots. You decide what properties to buy and what improvements to make.

> **You might be able to tap into your retirement account to fund real estate investments.**

For more information on this tax-deferred technique, visit Equity Trust Company at www .trustetc.com.

How to Escape Income Taxes   As noted, owner-occupants can flip a home every two years and pocket up to $250,000 of capital gains tax free ($500,000 for married couples filing jointly).[1] (Also, homeowners typically can obtain financ-ing on better terms and at lower costs than investors.) Tax-free gains for owner-occupied properties represent one of the best breaks available under the tax code. Take advantage of it.

As noted, investors who do not occupy their properties can es-cape income taxes on the profits they earn from property improvements and appreciation—at least during the time that they're building a portfolio of properties. To achieve this goal, use a Section 1031 exchange. With a 1031 exchange, you (with-in a specified period) sell your property and buy another one.[2] Your entire equity counts toward

> **Use a tax pro to reduce your taxes.**

---

[1]Under the "unforeseen circumstance" (e.g., job change, divorce, ill health) rule, the IRS may permit you to realize a tax-free gain even though you sell your home before two years have elapsed.

[2]Generally, you must complete the total transaction within 45 to 180 days. Consult your exchange pro for the details as they would apply to the timings of your specific property acquisition and sale.

the down payment for your new purchase. Over a period of 8 to 12 years, some investors have used the Section 1031 rule multiple times to exchange from a starter $100,000 property up to a $10,000,000 property—all tax free!

Profit Formula in Action

In later chapters, we discuss each item in the profit formula. You learn how to arrange financing, create value with improvements, effectively market the property to its target market, and raise money. Though, right now you may be most concerned with the challenges of the renovation process itself. So, here are the basic pointers to get the work done.

Getting the Work Done

You may have heard of remodeling "horror" stories, but if you adopt basic precautions you can keep your projects on schedule and within budget. To transform your entrepreneurial ideas into profits, here are the main issues:

- ◆ Know your limits.
- ◆ Distinguish the personal from the profitable.
- ◆ Plan your total project, and then work your project according to plan.
- ◆ Secure bids from dependable contractors and tradespeople.
- ◆ Eliminate the possibility of mechanic's liens.
- ◆ Obtain permits and comply with zoning and building codes.

Know Your Limits

Many renovators who get into difficulty stretch (or go beyond) their actual knowledge, time, money, or capacity to bear risk. The first point of vulnerability occurs with the enthusiastic beginner who rushes into a deal without a due diligence property inspection and informed cost estimates for repairs and improvements.

> **Try a few easy jobs first.**

A second point of vulnerability occurs after your first three or four successes. With success comes overconfidence (or even arrogance). You may tend to jump into projects for which experience has not prepared you. Or, you may skip some steps in due diligence because you say to yourself, "I know what I'm doing," or "This won't be a problem."

When I was learning to fly my own plane, I was told to memorize:

There are old pilots. There are bold pilots. But there are no old *and* bold pilots.

The same lesson holds true for real estate fix and flippers. As you approach each project you contemplate, weigh the requirements of the project against your capabilities. Use your first projects as learning experiences. Conservatively figure your MIV. Overestimate costs (time and money) as well as your *oops* factor. Negotiate tough on price. It is better to walk away from five potentially good deals than get in over your head in one disastrous project.

Distinguish the Personal from the Profitable

> **Homeowners often fail to create value because they "personalize" their renovations.**

Each year, *Remodeling* magazine features an article that presumes to tell homeowners how much "payback" they can expect to receive for various types of home improvement projects. Ignore their results (which are reported widely in newspapers and "home"-type magazines). Why? Because *Remodeling's* research does not distinguish *personal* home improvement projects from those undertaken by *professional profit-seeking* entrepreneurs.

What Difference Does It Make?   Recently, I stopped by a "for sale" house that was undergoing renovations. As I spoke with the (amateur) homeowner, she bubbled with enthusiasm over the $35,000 that she had just spent to remodel the kitchen in the house. Will she and her husband get back their money for this kitchen improvement? Not likely. Here's why:

1. *Piecemeal renovation.* The new kitchen no longer fit the old house. In fact, it looked out of place. When professionals remodel, they don't approach tasks piecemeal. They envision an end result in terms of total impact. Seldom can you take one part of a property to a level substantially above the rest and expect a profitable payback.

2. *Expensive materials without good design.* Although the kitchen looked good with its expensive Wood-Mode cabinets, Mexican tile floor, and upscale appliances, the work triangle was horribly ill designed. The stove top, range, and microwave were located 18 feet away from the kitchen sink across a wide expanse of floor area. Any professional knows that all major ingredients of a kitchen (fridge, work counter, ovens, sink, range) should be positioned for no more than a three-step triangle for ease of food preparation.

3. *"We've spent $35,000 . . ."* Amateurs frequently emphasize how much they've spent on renovations as if that amount automatically justifies a corresponding increase in value.

4. *Serious negatives remained uncorrected.* The house still retained its original (and functionally obsolete) awning-type crank windows and the view from the family room looked into an unlandscaped backyard and a neighbor's house located not more than 20 to 25 feet away. Again, in keeping with the principle of "total effect," a professional would allocate renovation dollars such that these negatives were cured. Seldom will isolated pizzazz sell, if basic flaws remain.

> **Never view improvements piecemeal. Create a total unified impact that will impress buyers (tenants).**

As so often happens, this amateur renovator got carried away with her *personal* vision for the kitchen.

Unfortunately, profitable paybacks do not coincide with *personal* visions that ignore market realities. Instead, they easily turn into money losers.

Professionals Market Test Their Ideas   Professionals never go forward with their ideas until they have tested them against talks with design experts, a survey of competitive properties and sales prices, and, yes, common sense (i.e., buyers' eyes). Professionals also explore their ideas with top realty agents who frequently list and sell properties in the neighborhood. Allocate your dollars wisely. Discipline personal enthusiasms with market reality. Buyers pay for benefits they value. They do not reimburse homeowners or investors for the costs of their personal enthusiasms or idiosyncratic ideas.

> **Your plan spells your success.**

Plan Your Project, Work Your Plan

Before you begin, create a detailed renovation plan for the entire property:

1. *Budget priorities.* Allocate your renovation dollars across the total project such that you will receive the biggest bang for the buck. Only after you've planned the total work can you realistically trade off and prioritize. The frequently voiced approach of "we might as well get started on this now and figure out the rest later" lays a sure path to regret.
2. *Sequencing.* When you proceed *without* a complete plan in view, you waste time and money. Some early work will need to be redone, you will lose potential economies of scale, and you throw away materials early on that actually could have been used later—if only you had thought about it. A fully developed plan helps you sequence and coordinate your work to achieve optimum results.
3. *Change orders.* Some contractors bid their jobs low and make their profits on change orders. They know that many renovators (especially amateurs) follow the "we can decide that later" approach, and deciding later means that renovators lose their

power to negotiate and obtain competitive bids. The contractor can price change orders for maximum profit (his or her profit, of course, not yours).

4. *"As long as . . ."* A sketchy plan also brings about the three most costly words in renovation, "as long as. . . ." You know, "As long as we're now doing this, we might as well. . . ." If you want cost overruns, make "as long as" your standard operating procedure.

5. *Avoid trade wars.* If you live in a strongly union area, be aware that, on occasion, jurisdictional wars break out on jobs over which trade (plumbing, carpentry, electrical, etc.) is entitled to what type of work—often down to the slightest detail. A fully detailed plan can help ensure that potential disputes are headed off before they become trade union conflicts. Allocate work early on. Smooth out potential border quarrels.

> **Include your "As long as . . ." improvements into your original plan. Avoid add-ons.**

Granted, you never achieve perfection through advance planning. You will decide to modify, omit, or add to. Nevertheless, a comprehensive, upfront, detailed plan will serve you far better than the ad-hoc one-step-at-a-time approach. Profitable renovations do not proceed according to the whim and fancy of the moment. They proceed according to thoughtful priorities, sequencing, scheduling, and budgeting.

Secure Bids

As you solicit bids for your jobs, your possible choice of contractors, subcontractors, tradespeople, and handymen will run into the hundreds. (But, of course, the same can be said for nearly every trade or profession.) So, before you secure a bid, set credibility criteria for the people whom you consider for the job(s). Then, verify that all bids cover the same scope of work, competency, quality of materials, and guarantees. Finally, select the best value (not necessarily the lowest) bidder.

> **You can achieve top quality with low bids.**

Establish Credibility   It does little good to secure bids from persons who either can't or won't fulfill your renovation agreement. How can you assure yourself of bidder credibility? Try the following:

◆ Ask around. Obtain referrals from people you know. Since home remodeling has become one of our chief American pastimes, this approach will generally turn up some good candidates. You can also obtain referrals from home supply stores, the yellow pages, and the classified and display ads in newspapers.

◆ Once you gather names, interview the people. Obtain additional job references, credit information, and work history. Determine whether the potential bidders can start and complete your job within your time/cost budget.

◆ Confirm that the person is licensed, bonded, and insured. Except for relatively small cosmetic or cleanup work, you avoid those who work "off the books" or in some other ways skirt the responsible operating procedures of a reputable business.

> **Compare competitive bids. Do they include precisely the same labor and materials (scope of work)?**

Scope of Work   As you solicit bids, make sure that all contractors include the same scope of work and quality of materials. You don't want to walk around the house with a bidder and say things like, "We're going to want these rooms painted; we'll need new flooring here and over there; and we want the kitchen cabinets replaced, and maybe change that light fixture."

In terms of preliminary ballpark discussions, you might rely on loose discussions to get you thinking about the work you actually want to consider. But to accurately compare—and to prevent controversy about exactly what work the bid covers—every bidder must understand precisely what they're bidding on.

In instances when you haven't decided on brand, model, and color (or similar types of decisions), investigate typical prices. Then specify an "allowance" factor in the bid. Or alternatively, request the bid with an "owner will provide" exception.

Compare Bids and Bidders   In addition to scope of work, ask contractors to submit their bids in similar line-item detail. Be wary of gross bids, that is, bids that fail to itemize costs (e.g., kitchen remodeling—$12,627).

The detailed, line-item bid helps you in four ways:

1. *Verify comparability.* Without detail, you can't know for sure that the bids cover the same scope of work and quality of materials.
2. *Question, question.* Use the bid process to learn what, how, and why. The more you understand, the better you will become at finding and designing the most profitable renovations.
3. *Negotiate, negotiate.* When you compare line items among contractors, you will likely find some wide differences. To a certain degree, you can use low estimates from one contractor to justify a cost reduction from another. "I'm leaning toward you for this job, but you show $2,800 to move that wall and replace the windows. If you were to get the job, do you think you could do it for $1,800? That's the price others have quoted."
4. *Cherry picking.* Some hardball renovators "cherry pick" their contractors. They ferret out the itemized low-cost items from several bidders and award multiple jobs accordingly. Some contractors reject this ploy. If you try it, you may destroy good will and lose a good contractor. At times, though, you could give it a shot.

> **You get what you *bargain* for.**

Once the bids are in and you've questioned and negotiated, whom do you choose? If you're certain that you've established credibility and comparability, then I see no reason to choose the mid- to high-cost bidders. In my experience, the adage, "you get what you pay for"—which implies the lower the price, the lower the quality—has not proven true.

That doesn't mean I always select the low bidder. For I also want someone who communicates well, coherently explains answers to my questions, and displays a fair sense of give and take. When a bidder combines these attributes with lower costs, he or she has won the job (subject only to memorializing our full agreement in writing).

Secure Lien Releases

Persons or firms who supply labor or materials for property improvement may file a lien against that property—if that supplier doesn't get paid in full for his or her contribution to the improvement project. Say you pay your contractor 100 percent of all amounts agreed. But your contractor doesn't pay the company where he bought the roof shingles that are now affixed to your house. That unpaid supplier of the shingles can look to you for payment.

You can claim, "I paid the contractor, go collect from him," but to no avail. The same principle holds for those painting, electrical, and plumbing subcontractors who worked on your property. If the contractor doesn't pay them, (under most state laws) you must—or suffer a lien on the property and a cloud on its title.

The Solution   At the time you pay your prime contractor, request that he complete and sign an unconditional waiver and release form. (To secure an *unconditional* release, you may need to pay with a cashier's check—otherwise the contractor may give you a *conditional* release that will mature into an unconditional release once your personal check is cleared by the bank.) In addition, require your contractor to submit copies of unconditional lien releases from each subcontractor and supplier.

> **Secure lien releases.**

Because mechanic's lien laws vary by county, state, and country, check with a local attorney to find the procedures that protect you in the legal jurisdiction where your property is located. But regardless of where you are located, never pay for work to your property without simultaneously obtaining a written lien release.

Buyer Beware   Now let's view the lien problem from the buyer's perspective. Say you offer to buy a property that shows off a brand-new exterior paint job. Your lender obliges your request for a fast closing. In just three weeks, the deal's done. Shortly thereafter, you receive notice that a painting contractor has slapped a lien against what is now *your* property.

You complain to the unpaid contractor, "Wait a minute, you can't do that. Go after the previous owner. I didn't have anything to do with that paint job." But again, your complaint falls on deaf ears. To clear the title to the property, you must pay the painter. In turn, you can go after the seller for reimbursement. Maybe you will get your money back; maybe you won't.

> **Be wary of properties with recent repairs or improvements. Ask to see lien releases for all recent work.**

Still, one fact remains. Mechanic's liens are levied against a property, not a person. To protect yourself as a buyer, ask for copies of the seller's lien releases for any work to the property (just to be safe) that has occurred during the preceding 12 months.

Stay Legal: Obtain All Necessary Permits and Comply with All Zoning and Building Codes

Some foolish renovators take the view, "We don't need no stinking permits." But you do need all required permits and to comply with all zoning laws and ordinances. In days gone by, do-it-yourselfers, cheapskate renovators, and bootleg contractors ignored such laws with reckless abandon and yet incurred little risk.

Today, most governments no longer tolerate this behavior. Just as importantly, most buyers now employ professional inspectors who note nonconforming work. A contractor might tell you,

"Oh, you don't need to bother with all of that bureaucratic red tape. I can do that work without a permit and save you money. You will need to pay me in cash for the job. That's not a problem, is it?" *Run* from this ploy. When a bootleg contractor screws up, who's responsible? You are! So, stay legal. To that topic we now turn in more detail.

CHAPTER 4

Make Regulations Work for You

> **Savvy renovators learn the laws and profit from the loopholes.**

In the world of real estate, you can't escape regulation[1] When you buy, finance, renovate, own, lease, use, manage, convert, or sell property, you need to learn the rights, remedies, restrictions, and yes, opportunities that such rules create. Yet, nearly all books on flipping and fixing, as well as those that deal (more generally) with real estate investing, ignore this vital topic.

Widespread ignorance of regulation leads to five types of serious errors:

1. *Missed advantage.* As an entrepreneur, you want to renovate, manage, and sell your properties to create the highest profits. But, without detailed knowledge of what you can and cannot legally do, you miss profitable possibilities; or you might incorrectly assume that you can make some changes that in fact the law prohibits.

2. *Purchase errors.* Prior to purchase, learn whether the property conforms to all applicable rules. Without this knowledge, you may find that you must spend for updates that catch you by

---

[1]Of course, in today's world, virtually no activity of consequence escapes regulation. In this respect, real estate fits the norm.

surprise. If that enclosed porch or converted attic doesn't comply with the regulations, it's you who may have to pay to tear
out these illegal improvements and rebuild according to code.

3. *Mistakes in use.* Land-use rules not only create exclusive (and
    inclusive) zoning districts (commercial, residential, industrial),
    such regulations may also govern occupancy, signage, parking,
    home occupations, noise, yard care, and even whether you (or
    your tenants) can put up a basketball hoop or hang clothes on
    an outdoor clothesline.

4. *Mismanagement of rentals.* Federal, state, and local laws may
    govern anything from security deposits to discrimination to
    eviction. Failure to follow lawful rules and procedures can sub-
    ject you to fines or liability claims.

5. *Sales and leasing miscues.* Not only do laws prohibit certain
    defined types of intentional discrimination, rules may also gov-
    ern print advertising, property disclosures, and for-sale (for-
    rent) sign size and placement.

To win the game of real estate, follow the rules, try to get the rules
changed, or seek a lawful exception. All too often, I hear investors and
homebuyers rail against the rules of government or the rules of their
homeowners associations (HOAs). Yet, the rules complained of were in
effect at the time these people bought. They had failed to investigate.

> **Learn the rules and you can play a winning hand.**

Can you imagine sitting down for a game of
poker, joining a foursome for a round of golf, or step-
ping onto a squash court, racquet in hand—without
first learning the rules of the game? No; it doesn't make
sense, does it? Unless you don't care to win. But if you
do care to come out ahead, do what many investors
fail to do. Study the government, private, and contrac-
tual rules that govern your property (or the property that you're evaluating
to buy). Your superior knowledge pays off in two ways: (1) You capitalize
on profitable opportunities that others miss, and (2) you steer around those
pitfalls and roadblocks that cause others grief and misfortune.

This chapter highlights the rules that may apply to the properties
you buy. Though space does not permit a detailed presentation, this

introduction guides you toward the sources and types of regulations that you will encounter.

Sources of Regulations

Here are the main sources of restrictions that may govern your properties:

◆ Governments (federal, state, county, city)
◆ Homeowners associations
◆ Private contracts such as mortgages, insurance policies, and easements

> **Use the rules to control the neighborhood riffraff.**

Note, too, these restrictions don't just govern *your* property. They govern your neighbors and your tenants. Often, you can enlist various rules to stop others from acting in ways that run down the value of your property. When sensible, rules protect and enhance property values.

Governments

The authority of local government to regulate a property generally depends on where a property is located. However, locations aren't always what they seem. Sometimes people buy property just outside the city limits to escape high taxes or strict zoning. Then, they find that the city still maintains authority over them. Sometimes, cities regulate a mile or more beyond city limits.

This same principle applies to coastal zoning and land use. Logic says that coastal zoning applies only to coastline properties. But the law may extend more broadly. Even school districts may not govern where you assume. Some homebuyers bought homes in an area of Highland

**Look closely
to learn which
governments and
what agencies
regulate a
property.**

Park, Texas, only to learn later that their kids must attend Dallas public schools rather than those of the more prestigious Highland Park. One of my previous homes carried a Berkeley, California, address, yet the property was subject to the zoning laws and building codes of Oakland, California.

To understand applicable laws, question which government jurisdictions, departments, and agen-cies can reign over you and your property. The answer might surprise you.

Who Administers and Enforces the Rules?   Have you ever danced the government runaround? It's not fun. But sometimes you must. "We don't handle that. You'll have to see. . . ."

When dealing with regulatory issues, you might have to shuttle back and forth among various agencies and departments of government. What's the answer? Persistence and knowledge. If you encounter this type of runaround, don't give up. Especially when you're trying to enforce a rule against a neighborhood scalawag, government clerks may claim that (1) it's not their responsibility; (2) you must first fill out six pages of forms in triplicate; or maybe (3) "yes, the offense falls within our domain, but we just don't have the time or the personnel to follow up on these types of complaints."

Don't accept these types of answers. Press persistently (but gently) for the results you want. If there is still no positive response, write the elected official who ultimately exercises responsibility over

**Ask a judge
to force
neighborhood
violators to
clean up their
properties.**

that department. Send copies to both the department head and the clerk(s) in question. In severe cases, ask a judge to issue a writ of mandamus. (Do you remember *Marbury vs. Madison*?) In issuing a writ, the judge can order government officials to enforce the law. (Similarly, you can also get a judge to force members of an HOA to comply with the association's declarations, bylaws, and rules. This possibility is discussed later in the chapter.)

Back Up Persistence with Knowledge To learn land-use laws, you can now access most local, state, and federal laws as well as judicial opinions over the Internet (e.g., www.municode.com or www.lexis.com). As another possibility, talk with property owners and investors. Find out their experiences in working with regulatory personnel. Learn how they cut through the red tape. Also, consult a lawyer who specializes in property regulatory issues (not the typical real estate lawyer who drafts contracts and shuffles papers at mortgage closings). A lawyer who routinely works with the regulatory agencies can provide you with a wealth of valuable information about how the regulatory world works in your area.

> **Use a lawyer with specialized knowledge of local zoning practices.**

Use this insider knowledge to get what you want and to figure out ways to avoid, minimize, or alleviate those regulations that work against your interests. Persistence notwithstanding, it pays to pick your battles. Insider knowledge can help you choose when to fight and when to move on to more productive and profitable ways to invest your time and money. Insider knowledge about regulatory issues can steer you away from losing efforts before you buy a property in hopes of combating regulatory compliance, enforcement, change, or exception.

I know of many investors and homebuyers who just assumed that they could get a variance that would permit them to make the improvements they wanted. That assumption has often proved wrong. Always verify. Never rely on the assertions of a seller or sales agent who says, "Oh, that shouldn't be a problem. You can just get a variance to cover it."

> **Homeowners associations can control more tightly than governments.**

Homeowners Associations

Too many people buy properties without fully investigating the fiscal and regulatory controls levied by their condo, co-op, and subdivision associations. These HOAs tax and regulate just as governments do. As a property owner within an association, you must either pay your assessed fees and abide by all properly enacted rules or you will suffer fines and even a potential foreclosure of your property. Not only can HOAs take these steps against property owners but they can enlist the power of the courts and sheriff to enforce them. And if the association itself does not act, any individual member (property owner) within the association has legal standing to bring suit for enforcement or compliance.

What Types of Regulations?   HOAs may regulate everything that government regulations control—but often in greater detail and with less judicial review. In addition, some HOAs limit your right to sell or lease your property. Do not ever agree to buy a property that's governed by an HOA until after you read the association's rules, regulations, and restrictions.

HOA Solvency, Fees, Assessments, and Fines   HOAs levy fees and assessments to maintain and enhance the community. However, some associations do mismanage their finances. They fail to put aside enough money to pay for repaving the parking lots, replacing the roofs, or repairing the tennis courts, club house, and swimming pool. Then, to cover these fast-approaching financial shortfalls, the association boosts monthly HOA fees and maybe even assesses property owners special charges that can climb into the thousands of dollars.

If you don't pay these charges, the association can place a lien against your property. If you still don't pay, the association can obtain a court order that permits the sheriff to auction your property to the highest bidder.

> Some HOAs enjoy the power to fine homeowners who violate the HOA rules.

If you (or your tenant) repeatedly fail to comply with the HOA rules, the HOA can fine you. Sometimes these fines accrue for each day the violation persists. I've seen legal cases where obstinate (and foolish) homeowners have ended up paying fines in excess of $50,000.

Inspect the Resale Package   I'm not trying to discourage you from buying a property that's ruled by an HOA. With more than 30 million homeowners and tenants now living in such privately regulated communities, these homes have gained market share as a way of life. But it's not a way of life that all investors and homeowners appreciate.

Before you commit, closely review the HOA's resale package of governing documents. Do the association CC&Rs blend with your intent for the property?[2] Does the association management effectively budget to cover present and future operating and capital costs? What amount of monthly fees must you pay? Are any special assessments looming over the horizon? Does the HOA tend to fine homeowners excessive amounts for petty violations? Answer these questions. Then decide whether the property will prove to be a good investment. (For a thorough discussion of HOAs, see my book, *Make Money With Condominiums, Townhouses, and Coops*, Wiley, 2003.)

Sometimes you can create value by investing in condo or townhouse developments that are ruled by incompetent or lax HOAs. Then, band together with other concerned owners and spearhead a drive to turn the HOA around and consequently the project itself.

Private Contracts Also Restrict Property Owners

Will you finance your property with a mortgage? Are you going to buy an insurance policy? Both of these private contracts will regulate how you use your property. In addition, easements might also limit use.

Mortgage Restrictions   Unknown to most borrowers, lenders typically place several property-use clauses into their loan contracts that require you to:

1. Maintain the property in good repair.
2. Obtain the lender's written permission before remodeling or making other substantive changes to the property.
3. Occupy the property for at least 12 months—or otherwise arrange for higher-cost investor financing (see Chapter 12).

---

[2]CC&Rs refer to the covenants, conditions, and restrictions that govern the community's homeowners.

4. Assign all rents from the property (if it's a rental and you've defaulted on your mortgage obligations) to the lender.

As standard operating procedure, lenders do not rigorously enforce any of these clauses except in three types of situations: (1) You're impairing the value of the property because you're letting it run down, (2) you've got a warped idea about how to make improvements, or (3) you fibbed to the lender on your loan application. In these cases, lenders will enforce their right to immediately call your loan due.

> **Before you renovate, check the fine print of your mortgage.**

Property Insurance   Insurers do not write their policies to cover a property per se. Instead they cover named risks under certain detailed conditions for named insureds. For example,

1. *Occupancy.* If you change from owner-occupied to tenant-occupied, you must change your policy and policy coverages.
2. *Vacant.* If you leave the property unattended or unoccupied (check your policy for exactly how long), coverage automatically lapses.
3. *Remodeling and renovation.* If you're going to renovate or remodel a property (as opposed to merely paint, recarpet, and clean up), notify your insurer. You may need to amend your coverage prior to beginning work.
4. *Safety standards.* Verify that your renovations will not violate the insurer's safety standards (materials, building techniques, inadequate design).
5. *Use.* Never change the use of a property (single-family to additional living units, residential to office) without notifying your insurer.

Before you buy, discuss your intent for the property with an insurance agent. Get rate quotes for coverages. Then, after you close title, inform your agent of changes in your plans. Breach a clause, restriction, or

Before you renovate, check the fine print of your insurance policy.

condition in your insurance policy and your insurer may lawfully refuse to pay for any loss that your property suffers (even if unrelated to your breach).

Easements   Many properties are restricted by one or some combination of easements. Generally, these easements may give the city, the county, or a utility company the right to place electrical power lines; gas, water, or sewer pipes; alleys; or sidewalks across your property. Although you can use the property in any lawful way that you choose, you cannot do anything that interferes with the rights of the easement holder.

Creative design turned an "unbuildable" site into a lot for a new home.

Easement Creates Opportunity for Profit   I once bought a potentially valuable residential lot for a pittance because the seller thought the lot was unbuildable. Many years before, the seller had sold the county an easement to place a water runoff pipe lengthways through the center of the property at a depth of five feet. A 10-foot-wide easement gave the county perpetual access to the pipe.

However, sensing opportunity, I looked at the lot differently. I knew that in coastal areas, land-use regulations no longer allow property owners to build houses with living areas at sea level. To get around this restriction, owners build their homes on stilts (pier and beam foundation). If you've visited any coastal areas, you've probably seen this type of construction technique.

So, prior to buying the lot that was restricted by the easement, I checked to verify that I could use a similar idea to keep the drainage pipe accessible, yet still permit a house to be built. The answer came back affirmative. Rather than leave the first-story access area open, though, I partially enclosed it for storage and parking. When completed, the exterior looked attractive, but actually consisted of non-load-bearing removable walls that preserved maintenance access to the underground pipes.

Two Lessons   This example illustrates two important themes: (1) Closely verify all property restrictions before you buy, and (2) use entrepreneurial thinking to figure out ways to change, modify, alleviate, or get around restrictions if doing so will boost the profit potential of the property.

Many easements do not impair title. You could (as many people do) settle at closing and never realize that the property you've bought is subject to such a restriction. Don't make that mistake. Prior to purchase, walk the site to see the placement of any easements that may impede your use of the property. In most (but not all) cases, easement holders must record their rights in the courthouse land records office. Your title insurer can provide you with this information.

Zoning and Related Ordinances

Since the 1930s, zoning and other related property ordinances have steadily increased their coverage in scope and detail. To understand how

> **Zoning laws tailor specific rules to specific districts.**

such laws may apply to a property that you're looking at, consult local ordinances. Or preempt this issue. Consult the area's zoning map and relevant governing rules and regulations. Once you locate those neighborhoods that are zoned appropriately, look for properties that legally fit within your entrepreneurial plans.

The District Concept

To set up zoning laws, land-use planners design zoning maps that lay out multiple districts that may range in size from one small parcel of land up to several square miles or more. Sometimes, small zoning districts lie within larger districts—as when a small office complex or convenience retail center is surrounded by residences. In a few instances, small elite cities may zone the entire community all one district (typically, large-lot, single-family residential).

As Figure 4.1 shows, planners set forth multiple kinds of zoning districts. To see what zoning applies to a specific property, look up the

Article IV. Use Regulations

Division 1. Generally

Sec. 30-41. Establishment of zoning districts and categories.
Sec. 30-42. Designation of district boundaries.
Sec. 30-43. Rules for interpretation of district boundaries.

Residential Zoning Districts

Sec. 30-51. Single-family residential districts (RSF-1, RSF-2, RSF-3, and RSF-4).
Sec. 30-52. Residential low-density districts (RMF-5, RC, and MH).
Sec. 30-53. Multiple-family medium-density residential districts (RMF-6, RMF-7, and RMF-8).
Sec. 30-54. Residential mixed-use district (RMU).
Sec. 30-55. Residential high-density districts (RH-1 and RH-2).
Sec. 30-56. General provisions for residential districts.
Sec. 30-57. Residential leases; teaching of the fine arts.
Sec. 30-58. Home occupation permits.

Office Zoning Districts

Sec. 30-59. Office districts (OR and OF).
Sec. 30-60. General provisions for office districts.

Business and Mixed-Use Zoning Districts

Sec. 30-61. General business district (BUS).
Sec. 30-62. Automotive-oriented business district (BA).
Sec. 30-63. Tourist-oriented business district (BT).
Sec. 30-64. Mixed-use low-intensity district (MU-1).
Sec. 30-65. Mixed-use medium-intensity district (MU-2).
Sec. 30-66. Central city district (CCD).
Sec. 30-67. General provisions for business and mixed-use districts.

Industrial Zoning Districts

Sec. 30-68. Warehousing and wholesaling district (W).
Sec. 30-69. Limited industrial district (I-1).
Sec. 30-70. General industrial district (I-2).
Sec. 30-71. General provisions for industrial districts.

Special Use Districts

Sec. 30-72. Agriculture district (AGR).
Sec. 30-73. Conservation district (CON).
Sec. 30-74. Medical services district (MD).
Sec. 30-75. Public services and operations district (PS).
Sec. 30-76. Airport facility district (AF).
Sec. 30-77. Educational services district (ED).
Sec. 30-78. Corporate park district (CP).

Overlay Districts

Sec. 30-79. Historic preservation/conservation district.
Sec. 30-80. Special area plan district (SAP).

(continued)

Figure 4.1   Common Types of Rezoning Districts.

Figure 4.1   *(Continued)*

location of the property on the zoning map. After learning the relevant district category, read the corresponding explanatory section within the zoning ordinance to learn the precise regulations.

For example, if a property were located in this city's residential mixed use (RMU) district, turn to Section 30-54 of the zoning manual. If from the zoning map you see that the property is located in an RSF-4 district, you would consult Section 30-51.

What Types of Restrictions?

Zoning and related ordinances can control about anything you do outside of the privacy of your own bedroom. Some cities (such as Palm Beach, Florida, or Mill Valley, California–Marin County) regulate everything that's possible as tightly as possible. Other cities (such as Orlando, Florida) adopt a more eclectic approach. In Gilcrest County, Florida, it

◆ Type of property use	◆ Party walls
◆ Special uses/exceptions	◆ Obnoxious behavior
◆ Setback dimensions (front and rear)	◆ Smoke, dust, pollution
◆ Sideyard dimensions	◆ Aesthetics/architectural review boards (ARBs)
◆ Floor area ratio (FAR)	◆ Occupancy
◆ Lot coverage ratio	◆ Home occupations
◆ Building height	◆ Home businesses
◆ Parking	◆ Trespass
◆ Noise	◆ Fences
◆ Light	◆ Crowds
◆ View	◆ Historical districts
◆ Trees and shrubbery	◆ Yard care, weeds
◆ Accessory apartments	◆ Health and safety
◆ Swimming pools	◆ Solar panels
◆ Subdivision layout	◆ Signage
◆ Animal control	◆ Environment and ecology

Figure 4.2   A Sampling of Concerns for Zoning.

> **In some areas, almost "anything goes." In others, the government must approve a new mailbox.**

seems like you can drop a mobile home about anywhere you want without much fear of legal challenge. Right next door in Alachua County, sites permissible for mobile homes are much tougher to find.

The following discussion gives you a good idea of these rules that control property investors, renovators, and remodelers.

Setbacks, Sideyards, and Height Virtually all zoning ordinances tell property owners that they can't put their buildings too close to the street, their neighbors, or the neighboring site in the rear. What's too close? What buildings? It all depends.

Dimensions Look at Figure 4.3. You can see the requirements for four different residential single family (RSF) classifications in one town. Except for the maximum height requirements of 35 feet, the other dimensional standards *do not* represent "typical." No typical exists. Until the zoning law was changed, Vancouver, British Columbia, permitted some lots for RSFs at a width of 16 feet, sideyards of 2 feet, and front setbacks of 10 feet. In Barrington Hills, an expensive suburb of Chicago, minimum lot sizes require five acres. Some planned unit developments (PUDs) permit zero lot lines, as do some city townhouses and tenements. (Note: The du/a shorthand stands for dwelling units per acre.)

Buildings, Structures, Site Improvements, and So Forth When you check the requirements for setbacks and sideyards, notice what buildings or structures must comply. Zoning rules may permit screened porches, freestanding storage sheds, swimming pools, decks, garages, and driveways to sit closer to the property lines. With such exceptions common, you may enjoy more room for improvements than a casual glance at the requirements might imply.

> **Setbacks do not necessarily apply to all types of buildings and site improvements.**

Principal Structures				
	RSF-1	RSF-2	RSF-3	RSF-4
Maximum density	3.5 du/a	4.6 du/a	5.8 du/a	8 du/a
Minimum lot area	8,500 sq. ft.	7,500 sq. ft.	6,000 sq. ft.	4,300 sq. ft.
Minimum lot width at minimum front yard setback	85'	75'	60'	50'
Minimum lot depth	90'	90'	90'	80'
Minimum yard setbacks:				
Front	20'	20'	20'	20'
Side (interior)	7.5'	7.5'	7.5'	7.5'
Side (street)	10'	10'	7.5'	7.5'
Rear	20'	20'	15'	10'
Maximum building height	35'	35'	35'	35'

Accessory Structures,[1] Excluding Fences and Walls	
Minimum front and sideyard setbacks	Same requirements as for the principal structure.
Minimum yard setback, rear[2]	7.5'
Maximum building height	25'
Transmitter towers	80'

1. Accessory screened enclosure structures whether or not attached to the principal structure may be erected in the rear yard as long as the enclosure has a minimum yard setback of three feet from the rear property line. The maximum height of the enclosure at the setback line shall not exceed eight feet. The roof and all sides of the enclosure not attached to the principal structure must be made of screening material.

2. One preengineered or premanufactured structure of 100 square feet or less may be erected in the rear and side yards as long as the structure has a minimum yard setback of three feet from the rear or side property lines, is properly anchored to the ground, and is separated from neighboring properties by a fence or wall that is at least 75 percent opaque.

Figure 4.3 Dimensional Requirements for Residential Single Family (RSF) Districts.

Also, notice whether the law specifies where and how to take dimensional measurements. One statute I've seen measures height from street level. If your site slopes down, your structure could actually exceed 35 feet from ground level (if that were the maximum height). You can face measurement ambiguity, too, when your site boundaries do not form a perfect rectangle. With an angular site, your building could meet the setback rules at one point, but violate them at another.

Floor Area and Lot Coverage Ratios   If you're planning to add living or storage space to the main structure, check to see whether the zoning code sets floor area ratios (FARs) or lot coverage ratios (LCRs) for the property. A FAR expresses the square footage of the structure as a percentage of the square footage of the lot:

$$\text{Floor area ratio (FAR)} = \frac{2,400 \text{ sq. ft. (building size)}}{8,500 \text{ sq. ft. (lot size)}}$$
$$\text{FAR} = 28.2\%$$

If the regulation set the FAR limit at, say, 35 percent, you could add 575 square feet of building (2975 potential less 2400 existing).

$$\text{Maximum floor area} = .35 \times 8,500 \text{ sq. ft.}$$
$$= 2,975 \text{ sq. ft.}$$

However, your plans might also have to fit within an LCR. To make sure that a structure leaves enough room for parking and yardspace, government might limit the footprint of the building to some specified percentage of the site size. If, as in the above example, zoning set the maximum LCR at 30 percent, you would have to add your space into a second story, rather than building out:

$$\frac{\begin{array}{l}38,500 \text{ sq. ft. (lot size)} \\ 30\% \text{ (LCR maximum)}\end{array}}{2,550 \text{ sq. ft. (maximum footprint)}}$$

> **Never assume you know the law. Quirks and loopholes run everywhere.**

Now, we ask another complicating question: What parts of the structure count towards the FAR and LCR ratios—basements, decks, porches, garages, driveways? There's only one way to find out—read the law. If the ordinance remains silent or seems ambiguous, talk with a land-use lawyer to see whether you can find (argue for?) a profitable loophole.

Occupancy Restrictions   I recently inquired about a single-family investment property that was up for sale. The seller told me that the house was rented to five college students for $2,500 a month. "Sounds pretty good," I said. Then, hoping to win some negotiating points, I pointed out that the city's occupancy code limited single-family rentals to three unrelated adults. Therefore, I couldn't pay what the seller was asking because I wouldn't risk a code citation that could cost me a substantial part of my income flow.

"No problem," the seller countered. "This house sits in a commercial district. Five students don't violate the code within this zoning district."

It turns out that on this issue, he knew more about the code than I did—at least as it applied to his property. Smart seller—he had anticipated code questions and had prepared factual and accurate responses. This was a refreshing change from most run-of-the-mill sellers and realty agents who don't bother to learn anything about the land-use codes—until a serious mistake teaches a hard lesson.

Single-Family Occupancy   I relate this example to show how important it is to know the code regardless of whether you're buying or selling. The code affects use and use greatly influences value. But it also illustrates how ordinances can regulate who and how many tenants you place in a property. Many cities discriminate against adults who wish to share housing. Although less true now than in the past, single-family zoning has literally limited occupancy to one *family* of persons related closely by blood or marriage. (This rule is applied strictly in some zoned areas of Dubai—where I am currently doing some work.)

> **Social policy and modern trends sometimes conflict with zoning rules.**

Modern Exceptions Due to lobbying by property owners, the changing nature of households, and court decisions, restrictions on occupancy have become less severe—especially with regard to senior adult congregate living facilities, foster care homes, shelter homes for abused spouses and children, and group homes for the emotionally or mentally handicapped. Nevertheless, as a general principle, courts have told planners that they can legally establish districts that exclude residents by age, household size, household composition, and, de facto, by household wealth and income.

Indeed, many communities that attract large populations of immigrants face serious problems of overcrowding—at least from the perspective of longtime residents. Typical middle-class families find that the house next door now provides shelter for three generations, four cousins, and a couple of boarders—for a total of 10 to 15 persons. Should zoning and occupancy codes prevent such high occupancy? Can code enforcers defend against charges of ethnic discrimination? The courts will decide these issues in coming years.

Parking "No on-street parking between the hours of 2:00 A.M. to 6:00 A.M." You might think that such neighborhood parking ordinances somehow relate to traffic issues. And sometimes they do. But frequently restricted parking hours indirectly control the population density of a neighborhood. How can 8, 10, or 15 occupants of a house find adequate parking without on-street parking? Park in the front yard? The zoning rules outlaw that, too.

> **Zoning laws may regulate all types of on-street and off-street parking.**

Too Many Cars Whether residential, retail, or office, local ordinances regulate off-street and on-street parking. Laws regulate the placement of driveways, curb cuts, and minimum-size parking lots to accompany specific uses (apartments, office buildings, shopping centers). If you add living units to a property (such as an accessory apartment, or perhaps split a large house into three or four apartment units), verify whether the law requires more on-site parking spaces.

Recreation (and Other) Vehicles   In Palo Alto, California, and the surrounding Silicon Valley, homes with legal space for RV parking command a price premium. Not because the RVers, themselves, are bidding up these properties, but because housing's so scarce that someone will pay $600 a month just to live in an RV. Could this strategy work in your area (albeit at probably a lower rental rate)? Just note that cities (and HOAs) do regulate the parking of RVs, boats, trucks, and trailers. In my neighborhood, no resident may park a car or truck in their driveway or in front of their house if it displays a commercial emblem or logo that may be seen by passersby.

Home Businesses/Home Occupations   Millions of people now work from their homes. So, these folks offer fix-and-flip entrepreneurs a good target market to aim at. This trend will continue to grow. But beware: Zoning rules regulate people who want to operate an office or run a business from their residence.

> When legal, home offices and home businesses offer good opportunities for renovators.

Questions to Answer   Does the zoning district of the property permit work at home as a right? If not, can you fit the property within a special exception category (see later discussion)? What rules apply to parking, the number of allowable customer visits, hours of operation, signage, business licenses, and dedicated space? To what extent could you legally modify the structure to accommodate the home office or business? Can you rent the office or business portion of the residence to someone who doesn't live there? Precisely what types of occupations or businesses will zoning permit?

Missed Opportunity   The majority of fixers and renovators miss this market. Depending on the specific ordinance, you might target any of the following:

- ◆ Writers
- ◆ Artists
- ◆ Accountants
- ◆ Lawyers
- ◆ Insurance agents
- ◆ Music instruction
- ◆ Financial planners

- ◆ Seamstress/tailors
- ◆ Beauty shop
- ◆ Network marketers
- ◆ Child care
- ◆ Answering service
- ◆ Auto repair
- ◆ Web-based business

This list samples a variety of small, independent occupations and businesses that proliferate in our free-agent nation. Learn what locations and what property features work best for one or more types of these free agents and you may find a lucrative niche of opportunity.

Special Uses   Typically, zoning districts permit certain uses as rights and other named uses as special exceptions. If designated a right, you can proceed with your plans without delay. As long as you comply with setbacks, height, and other governing details, zoning administrators must approve your intentions. If the use is classified within the special exception category, zoning officials could deny (or modify) your plans (see Figure 4.4). They would need to object because your use would harm the public interest or create adverse effects for neighboring property owners. You can challenge this objection. And if you end up in court, the judge will reverse the normal legal presumption that planners know best. Instead, the planners must prove through the greater weight of the evidence that their opinion should rule.

> **Even districts zoned single-family typically permit other types of property uses.**

Do not conclude that a residential, commercial, or industrial district necessarily excludes other uses. Read the ordinances.

Historical Properties   To preserve the heritage of communities, planners designate some properties or some areas of town as "historically significant." Unless you know what you're doing, avoid historically regulated properties.

District: Single-Family (R-1-AA)
Uses by Right

1. Single family houses
2. Customary accessory uses
3. Boat houses and boat docks
4. Foster homes
5. Adult congregate living facilities

Uses by Special Exception

1. Public or private schools
2. In-home professional offices
3. Churches
4. Tennis clubs
5. Guest cottages
6. Golf courses
7. Public swimming pools
8. Shelter homes

Figure 4.4   Uses by Right or Special Exception as per One City Zoning Ordinance.

Unless you renovate to fulfill an aesthetic avocation, avoid historically designated areas and properties.

Planners may force such property owners to pony up thousands of dollars to maintain or restore these properties. They will likely want to approve your choice of colors, building materials, and design.

If you want to demolish all or part of an historically designated building, Heaven forbid! When Ritz-Carlton tried to build a new hotel in Sarasota, Florida, it needed to remove or demolish an old house that stood on the site. Sarasota's Historical Preservation Board put the Ritz through four years

> **Is neighbor noise a problem? Use the law to eliminate it.**

of public hearings and legal brawls. Only after spending hundreds of thousands of dollars for the costs of lawyers and delays did the Ritz-Carlton finally receive approval for their plans. (In the end, the company paid to remove the "historically significant" structure to another location.)

If you lack the patience of Job and the money of Buffett, run from any property that falls (or could fall) under the rules of historical preservation.

Noise Ordinances   Most communities have enacted noise ordinances that restrict decibel levels within specified zoning districts. Such ordinances may set exact rating systems and the type of equipment that code enforcers will use to measure noise. Alternatively, code enforcers may rely on a "plainly audible" standard such as the following:

> Plainly audible means any sound or noise produced by any source . . . that can be clearly heard by a person using normal hearing faculties, at a distance of 200 feet or more from the real property line where the source of the sound or noise is originating.

As to radios, stereos, televisions, and musical instruments, noise ordinances often tighten their restrictive standard:

> No person shall operate, play, or permit the operation or playing of any radio, tape player, television, electronic audio equipment, musical instrument, sound amplifier, or other mechanical or electronic soundmaking device that produces, reproduces, or amplifies sound in such a manner as to create a noise disturbance *across a real property boundary.*

If a noisy neighbor makes it difficult for you to sell or rent one of your properties, don't start a personal neighbor war. Instead, insist that the code enforcer emphatically tell the offender to cease and desist.

Sunlight and Views As sunlight and views have become more important to property owners and tenants, some cities have retreated from hands-off policies. With the advent of solar energy and $50,000 (or more) price premiums for view properties, owners have begun to demand protection for their sunlight and scenery. Even so, the general rule remains: The law offers little or no recourse to owners whose properties get blocked by tree growth or new (renovated) construction.

> **Make sure your view properties enjoy *protected* views.**

If your neighbor can legally build a second story that will shade your property's backyard and block its spectacular view of the mountains, you will probably lack legal standing to complain. If sunlight or views contribute to the value of a property that you're planning to buy, do not assume that those features will continue to serve your buyers or tenants. Verify, verify, verify!

When Tiger Woods bought a home with great views of the Pacific Ocean, the sales agent emphasized to a reporter of the *Los Angeles Times* that Tiger gained a *protected view*. Like Tiger, if you expect sunlight or view, verify whether it's either legally or locationally protected from loss.

Be Wary of Nonconforming Uses

Quite often, properties within their respective districts do not meet all current zoning and building codes. Are these properties legal? Maybe, maybe not. If the property and its current use legally predate the code's restrictions, the property has probably been grandfathered. It's now classified as legal and nonconforming. In contrast, if the property has been altered or operated in ways that were never legal, that property is classified as nonconforming and illegal.

> **Nonconforming properties present an additional risk. Verify before you buy.**

Legal and Nonconforming Here are four reasons why you should pay less for a legal property that does not conform to current zoning and building ordinances.

No Right to Expand the Use With legal and conforming properties, you can add on to the building up to the full extent of the current regulations. With nonconforming properties, the law typically does not permit such liberty.

Say you own a legal, nonconforming combination retail store with a residence upstairs. Business is so brisk at the store that you want to complete a 500-square-feet addition. Currently the zoning district prohibits retail use. You're probably out of luck. Zoning rarely allows property owners to expand a nonconforming use. In one legal case, the owner of a legal, nonconforming single-wide mobile home wanted to replace it with a double-wide. The planners and the courts said no.

No Right to Extend the Life You tell the zoning officials, "Okay, I won't expand, but I want to completely modernize the store (or mobile home) both inside and out." Sorry. You're probably out of luck again. The officials want nonconforming uses to die as soon as possible. They don't want you to revitalize it.

No Right to Renew the Use Assume that for some reason you close this nonconforming store for 90 days. You then try to reopen. You may have erred. Under most zoning laws, you cannot renew a nonconforming use after it has been discontinued for some period of time (as specified in the ordinance). The shortest period I've seen is 30 days. The longest is two years.

> **Don't "abandon" a nonconforming use.**

True story: As a rehabber or renovator, attend closely to the way local ordinances and court decisions regulate legal, nonconforming uses and nonconforming properties. For example, an investor owned a legal, nonconforming duplex that was located in a single-family district. When coincidentally the tenants of both units moved out within one week of each other, the investor decided to renovate the entire property. Working part-time, he completed the job in four months.

Then, within two weeks of reletting both sides, the code enforcer cited him for violating the current single-family district zoning. (A disgruntled neighbor may have filed a complaint.) When the investor appealed, the zoning board of adjustment turned a deaf ear. The statute was plain: "A nonconforming use that is discontinued or abandoned for more than 90 days shall be permanently terminated." I would like to end this story here, but it actually gets worse.

A single-family home is allowed one kitchen. But this property now proudly displayed two newly remodeled kitchens. What happens now? The zoning authority forced the investor to rip out one of the kitchens and convert the building into a single-family house.

> **Don't blame others for your failure to learn the law.**

The moral: When I relate this example in my investment seminars, attendees launch into their own war stories about petty, zealous zoning bureaucrats. But that's not the point. In this case, as in so many others that provoke investor chagrin, the statute clearly states the law. You can't justly condemn a zoning official for enforcing code. Had this duplex investor read the law before he acted, he could have easily worked his renovation plans into compliance.

Learn the law, then work the law to maximum advantage. That's the lesson this story teaches.

Note: This investor also violated code by performing his renovation work without permits. Had he sought the required permits, the officials might have warned him about the risk he was taking. As to illegally extending the life of a nonconforming use, that issue never surfaced in this case. Nevertheless, I would bet that when the code enforcer saw the unpermitted renovation of a nonconforming use, he became one riled-up bureaucrat. At that point, he probably targeted this investor for a fall.

No Right to Repair or Rebuild   I was hard on the foolhardy duplex investor. So I'll balance that indictment with a lesson about legal, non-conforming properties that I learned from experience.

Early in my investing career, I owned a 60-year-old apartment building that was wired with an outdated (legal, nonconforming) 60-amp fuse box. The property suffered an electrical fire that required a $200 repair. However, the code inspector would not permit a repair to below-code wiring. He required a rewire of the entire building with

> **Property insurance doesn't cover updating a damaged property to code.**

a 100-amp electrical system with circuit breakers, which at that time cost $2,000. (Such a rewiring today would cost much more.)

Typically, property insurance does not pay for code upgrade. Why not? Because unless you buy special coverage (which is often not available at a reasonable cost), insurance policies only promise to reimburse for actual losses. So, absent a code upgrade policy rider, insurers won't pay the extra costs necessary to bring it in line with the latest building or zoning code.

Illegal, Nonconforming Use   The United States and Canada have at least 50 million houses, apartments, and commercial buildings that *illegally* fail to conform to various zoning and building codes. Bootlegged renovations, makeshift repairs, unpermitted remodeling, excessive occupancy, outlaw home businesses, and incompetent, lazy, or dishonest building inspectors all contribute to this massive noncompliance. In the city of Vancouver, British Columbia, for example, more than 100,000 homeowners rent out illegal basement suites.

Calculate the Risk   I do not advise you against buying an illegal, nonconforming property. I have owned many such properties and have never suffered serious loss because of it. However, do not buy without knowledge. Calculate the risks. Then factor those risks into your purchase price negotiations. Tell the seller, "Look, the ceiling in your add-on rec room stands at just 7 feet 6 inches. Code says 8 feet minimum. If the building inspectors discover this violation, they could force me to tear out the entire roof and rebuild it to comply."

"They Never Enforce Those Laws"   The seller's likely response: "How are they gonna find out? Besides, they never enforce those laws." Of course, they do find out in many different ways.

◆ What if you have a small fire or storm damage that requires a permit for repair and a follow-up inspection?

◆ What if a spiteful neighbor or tenant turns you in?
◆ What if you plan other permitted renovations that bring an inspector into your property?

Code enforcers can uncover illegal properties (or uses) in a dozen ways. Is the rec room roof visible from the street? Maybe it will catch the eye of a zealous inspector who's just passing by. As to enforcement, do not rely on the past "live-and-let-live" attitudes. Political winds change directions—especially when the infractions generate neighborhood ill will (occupancy, parking, appearance, noise, blocked views).

Typically, code enforcers do not look for trouble. Unless forced to act by complaint or politics, most inspectors don't go after property

> **Code enforcers can discover violations any time they're called to inspect a property or approve work permits.**

owners who aren't causing any noticeable harm to others. Usually in my community, landlords get cited for violating occupancy codes only when their tenants (or properties) incite neighborhood complaints.

As to your decision to buy an illegal, nonconforming property, balance the potential risks and benefits against the seller's bottom-line price. But be wary. Should your renovations and fix-up work require a code permit and inspection, stay financially prepared to remedy all code deficiencies (or at least those violations that fall within the authority of that inspector).

How to Challenge the Zoning Rules

If you feel that zoning rules impact a property too harshly, seek change or attack the zoning law itself. Generally stated, you can pursue a remedy in some combination of the following:

◆ Seek a variance.
◆ Petition for rezoning.
◆ Go to court.

Sometimes you can gain exception from the rules.

As a matter of right, property owners may request a variance when a zoning rule creates undue hardship. Typically, "I want to make more money" doesn't qualify as hardship. From the planner's perspective, that "hardship" qualifies as tough luck.

When planners speak of hardship, they mean some unique feature of a property that renders it difficult to use in what would otherwise be a legal manner. For example, say sideyard setbacks require 10 feet. Your lot line cuts at an angle. The front part of your planned addition sets 12 feet of width; but at the back, only 8 feet of width. Absent some serious objection by a nearby property owner, you would probably get your variance.

Planners, though, do not typically grant hardship exceptions if you've previously created or contributed to the problem. You cannot murder your parents and then beg for mercy from the court because you're now an orphan. This rule particularly holds when you knowingly buy a property that will not legally accommodate your plans. Then you request a hardship variance. Don't expect sympathy from the folks at City Hall. To combat this potential problem, place a zoning variance contingency clause into your purchase contract. Most sellers won't like it. But if the variance stands critical to your plans, avoid the risk of refusal unless the seller offers a sufficiently attractive price or terms.

No Precise Rules   In the days when the good ole' boys lorded over zoning departments, the politically connected and financially generous could get variances (and zoning changes) almost at will. Such practices still remain in some cities and counties. Nevertheless, variances (and rezoning) must not conflict with the governing district norms and the overall comprehensive plan for the community. Today, variances do not generally grant special privileges.

Whom you know still counts in code approvals.

Nevertheless, those "who, when, and why" issues still make the variance process somewhat personal and situation specific. No precise rules apply. If a variance will help you make more money, seek insider knowledge before you submit your request. Whom and how you ask for a variance can influence a thumbs-up or -down answer.

Petition for Rezoning   If your property is uniquely situated to benefit from a more profitable use, you can petition the planners to rezone your site. Say that due to a new nearby office development, increased traffic flows, or the evolving nature of the neighborhood, your building merits another zoning classification. Professional offices would now better fit this location.

Unlike a variance, which according to contemporary zoning theory should pertain only to adjusting a regulatory detail or two, rezoning puts you in another league with a new set of rules. Much like a variance, though, planners won't rezone your property unless you show how such a rezoning will not harm neighboring properties or the integrity of the overall community plan.

> **Enlist help to get the laws changed.**

Power in Numbers   If you can enlist other nearby property owners to join with you to register a joint request that covers multiple properties, you increase your chance for success. Make community-need arguments. And you can enlist the power of numbers to support your request. Often, property owners push for upzoning. Though in cases of community revitalization, residents may adopt a "Let's restore the family neighborhood" approach. If more, not fewer, restrictions could enhance property values, push for downzoning.

Boundary Dominoes   What if your single-family residential property sits on a zoning district boundary line? Say you're situated right in back of a Safeway parking lot. You think that you should at least get an R-1-C classification so that you could convert the house to an office for lease to an accountant, lawyer, or maybe a veterinarian. More than likely, the planners will refuse. They will cite the domino effect.

> **Anticipate and prepare to rebut objections.**

"If we shift the zoning on your property, then your neighbor, too, will deserve a change. Where will it all end?" Again, the power of numbers may assist your case. Remember, explain not only why the unique location of your property justifies the shift in zoning classifications, but also why (absent the power of numbers) your property's location and use doesn't adversely impact neighboring properties. Perhaps your closest residential neighbor sits on the other side of an alley behind a thick hedgerow that stands 18 feet tall. "As to the property across the street," you persuasively point out, "that's a small neighborhood park where people walk their dogs. So, you see, my property would make a great location for a veterinary clinic."

Go to Court   Nearly all zoning laws give property owners and concerned parties several levels of appeal within the system. If you strike out with front-line personnel, go to the department head, then to a zoning board of adjustment, and eventually perhaps to a city or county council. Should you fail at all of these levels, you alone (or with the power of numbers) can file suit.

You might sue to force government to treat you and your property in a way that better serves your interests. Or you might sue to block the rezoning or planned use of nearby land that will bear adversely on the value of your property as well as the health, safety, morals, or general welfare of the community. (Remember, whenever possible, work the community-needs angle into your argument. Ayn Rand notwithstanding, neither planners nor judges typically appreciate the virtue of selfishness.)

> **Position your request in terms of the public interest.**

High Cost   If you file suit, employ an attorney who specializes in land-use litigation. Zoning and land-use cases involve too much complexity for self-help law. As such, given the high cost of lawyers and litigation, small investors (by themselves) can rarely afford to use the judicial system to fight zoning battles in court (unless a "property rights" advocacy group sees enough merit and precedent-setting value to take on the court battle for you).[3]

---

[3]For example, the Pacific Legal Foundation has litigated many cases on behalf of small property owners.

Avoid Trouble   Because "I'll see you in court" doesn't really offer small investors a practical response to planners, I again urge you to learn the law before you act. To avoid trouble with the code enforcers, read your local laws; gain insider knowledge; and press your case with tact, diplomacy, and perseverance.

Building Codes

Up to this point, we haven't distinguished zoning and other types of land-use and occupancy codes from building codes. That's because no clear distinction prevails. A rule that falls under zoning in one local area could fall under the building codes in another. Sometimes, too, various government controls overlap.

> **Property owners who do their own work must still comply with permits and codes.**

Small investors primarily meet up with *building code* inspectors when performing (or contracting for) plumbing, electrical, remodeling, or roofing work. These building codes may force you to use construction techniques, designs, or materials that can add to your costs (generally for reasons of safety). But they will seldom seriously restrict basic plans for renovation and market strategy (as can zoning and other land-use ordinances).

Environmental Laws

Small investors and renovators may run into six types of environmental issues:

- Lead paint
- Asbestos
- Underground home heating oil tanks
- Septic systems and wastewater disposal
- Tree ordinances
- Mold

Tree ordinances may prohibit you from cutting down a tree on your property to make way for a room addition or maybe to enhance a view of the mountains or bay.

As to the serious and costly issues of lead paint, asbestos, mold, heating oil tanks, and waste disposal (if your property's not connected to a city or county sewer line), get copies of the pertinent brochures published by local, state, and federal environmental agencies. If you locate a property that requires removal or abatement of any of these types of environmental problems, get back into your car and look for another property unless you enjoy deep pockets and a high tolerance for risk.

Rarely should beginning renovators carry out an environmental cleanup. There is too much uncertainty for too little payback. Focus on value-enhancing opportunities—not remedial restorations.

CHAPTER 5

What Possibilities Can You Envision?

When James Young discovered a termite-infested, Washington Village row house with a charred interior and shaky foundation, he knew he had found the property he was looking for. Priced at $32,000, properties didn't come much cheaper. But James's two kids, Adam and Tenea, weren't impressed. "When they looked at the house," says James, "they said 'No way.' But I could envision the possibilities. The house had three stories and I knew I could do a lot with it. I told the kids to just be patient. They'd see."

Big profits can come from a destroyed property.

James's prophecy proved right. That wreck of a property now displays functional beauty and strong character. It includes a spiral staircase, exposed brick firewalls, large matched triangular clerestory windows, a new oak floor, a double-tiered Corinthian column on each side of the living room fireplace, a completely equipped contemporary-style kitchen, and a third-floor master-bedroom suite with skylight, fireplace, and roof deck. As for the kids, they enjoy the second floor to themselves with private bedrooms at each end of the hall. Total cost of the property plus rehab expenses came to $77,000 (not including James's labor). Total rehabbed value today exceeds $235,000.

The Copleys Make Half a Million

"As my husband pulled up in front of that confused amalgam of materials and architectural styles that had once been a proud and stately Edward Durrell Stone–designed home, I told him he was not even going to get me out of the car—let alone walk inside. That place was a bastardized disaster," remembers Virginia Copley. But Virginia's husband Carl persuaded Virginia to change her mind.

"That's why Carl and I complement each other so well," says Virginia. "He has the eye for turning a sow's ear into a silk purse." The Copleys bought this house that had sat on the market unsold for nearly five years. Its asking price was $3.25 million. The Copleys negotiated a purchase price of $1.35 million. With another $400,000, they restored the house to its original splendor and boosted its market value to $2.5 million.

> **Before you reject, envision possibilities.**

The Baglivis Discover a Bargain

Christine and Kevin Baglivi recently bought their first home. "The hardwood floors," says Christine, "were encrusted with chewing gum . . . [the previous owner's children] had smashed the bathroom tiles and practiced their artwork on the walls. . . . Every window sash was broken, kitchen drawers were missing, and the bathtub looked as if it had served as a storage bin for used auto parts.

> **In expensive markets, fixers boost chances for home ownership.**

"Why would two presumably sane adults purchase such a nightmare?" Christine asks rhetorically. "Because like many Californians priced out of the housing market, investing in a fixer-upper helped us break into Southland real estate at a time when we didn't think we could afford to buy. Our three-bedroom Craftsman bungalow cost $80,000 less than similar homes in the neighborhood that were in good condition. To Kevin and myself, this savings gave us our chance to own a home."

Put on Your Rose-Colored Glasses

Do you see the common theme in each of these success stories? With each property, the buyers put on their rose-colored glasses. They

> **Envision with rose-colored glasses.**

could envision possibilities where others saw only problems. As an entrepreneurial fixer, put on your rose-colored glasses. Instead of merely itemizing what's wrong with a property, ask, "What could I make right? How can I enhance this property in ways that others remain too dull to see?"

Don't Quickly Reject a "Fixer"—You Just Might Pass Up a Bargain

Many investors reject properties too quickly. They walk in, do a quick take with a pass-through tour, and then say something like, "Let's get out of here. It's way too dark; and did you notice that awful burnt orange carpeting in the bedroom?"

"Yes," the spouse replies, "and how about those ugly kitchen appliances and that green linoleum floor—not to mention the garbled floor plan and water stains on the ceiling. This house needs too much work. Anybody would be *crazy* to buy this nightmare."

Well, yes, anybody would be crazy to buy that property—unless, of course, one could buy it at a steep discount, rehab, redecorate, and sell it for a profit of $50,000 to $100,000. Or perhaps, if in buying a discounted fixer, buyers were able to move into a higher-priced neighborhood they otherwise could not afford. Then these buyers wouldn't be called crazy. They'd be called *smart*.

As I travel throughout the country and talk to investors and homebuyers, I'm amazed at the number of people I meet who have

Turn negatives into positives.	bought properties that had sat on the market for months, if not years. Yet, after buying properties that were rejected by dozens of other potential buyers, these folks transformed their sow's ear into a silk purse and earned profits of tens (sometimes hundreds) of thousands of dollars.

Your Second Set of Glasses (Buyer's Eyes)

Because a property sits unsold for months or years doesn't mean that it offers undiscovered promise. Many properties remain unsold because they're overpriced money traps. And that brings us to the next question: How can you weed out the money traps without rejecting the money-makers? For that task you need to bring along a second set of glasses. These glasses give you buyer's eyes. While wearing them, no flaw, short-coming, or defect escapes attention. You see each property detail in bright light.

The Critical Balance

As an entrepreneur, your rose-colored glasses help you to search for profit potential. Your buyer's eyes alert you to risks. To succeed as an entrepreneurial flipper/fixer, constantly switch from one set of glasses to the other. Then, as Ben Franklin suggested, tally the positives and the negatives. At that point, you make a fully balanced decision.

Use Ben Franklin's approach: List negatives and positives side by side.	**Uncommon Sense** This advice may seem like common sense. But in practice, it's not all that common. Unless you've got icewater running through your arteries, I guarantee that you're going to re-act emotionally to the neighborhoods and proper-ties you look at. The human animal tends to pick

up on some features of a property (good or bad) and then interprets everything else to fit that first impression.

Savvy Approach As you evaluate properties, sometimes you put on your rose-colored glasses and look for profit potential. At other moments, you take off the rose-colored glasses and put on those specs that force you to see with buyer's eyes. When you balance perspectives, you identify those lumps of coal that can become a treasured jewel to your prospective buyer (or tenant).

Inspecting a Site for Its Potential

To determine site potential, evaluate four major features:

1. Site size and configuration
2. Site quality (topography, landscaping, soil conditions)
3. Fencing, driveway, sidewalks
4. Curb appeal

Site Size and Configuration

Walk the boundaries of the property and measure each side. Follow the outline of a plat or survey that the seller provides you. If no plat or survey is available, ask the sellers to point specifically to where they believe the lot lines run. Use this site description in your preliminary measures. But before you buy, verify it.

> **Much of a property's value lies in the land.**

Why do you need to go to this much trouble? What difference does it make whether you know the exact size of the site and precisely where the boundaries lay?

What You See Isn't Necessarily What You Get Surprisingly, site size and configuration aren't always as they appear. Friends of mine who bought a home loved their big backyard that ran from the house 200 feet back toward a row of trees. But, in fact, the property's rear lot line did not correspond with the tree row as they had assumed. It actually lay 82 feet closer in. Their backyard was half the size they had originally believed it to be. They never checked the site's plat. They assumed that what they saw was what they got.

Walk the site's boundaries and you benefit in two other ways:

1. *Discover easements.* Remember, easements restrict use of a property. An ill-placed easement may prevent you from building on an addition, erecting a fence, or putting up a storage shed.
2. *Discover encroachments.* Does the neighbor's garage or driveway overlap the property line? Do any trees, shrubs, or fences appear to cross site boundaries?

> **Site boundaries influences the size, type, and positioning of potential improvements.**

If you discover potential problems, clear them before you spend for professional property inspections, repair estimates, mortgage application fees, an appraisal, or other property acquisition costs.

Improvement Plans: Regulatory Issues Remember those government regulations from Chapter 4 such as FARs (floor area ratios) and setbacks (sideyard, front yard, backyard)? When you measure the site size and locate boundary lines, you can figure whether you can legally add space, build a deck, or move a driveway. Many people buy properties with grand plans that push beyond the legal limits of their site.

Does the Site Give You an Extra Buildable Lot? "Where else but in Santa Fe," Realtor Dee Treadwell asks, "could you buy a home for $285,000, later subdivide the property, sell the house for $550,000, and still have a lot to sell?" Now, that's the kind of deal every investor wants to find. Yet, even though this Realtor seems not to realize it, you can

<blockquote>
Sites with extra buildable land give you "hidden value."
</blockquote>

find similar sites in every city throughout North America. Granted, Santa Fe's prices rank toward the high end. But if a structure sits across two or more lots, you can tear it down and sell the vacant lots individually. This means that if you buy a building that sits on several legally buildable lots, you might be looking at big *future* profits.

The key words here, though, are *legally buildable*. Just because a structure sits on a lot that's large enough to accommodate two or more newly built houses doesn't mean you can realize the site's profit potential. To reap the rewards, building regulations must permit you to split the land.

Combine Lots with a Neighbor   On occasion, a lot may include extra sideyard space but not quite enough to form a legally buildable site. In that case, look to an adjacent site. If you could persuade the owner of that property to sell you a 10-foot strip, you could then assemble enough plottage. Or with extra sideyard square footage, maybe you could put together enough land to create a duplex or triplex—when zoning allows it.

Keep Searching for More Profitable Uses for the Site   With accurate knowledge of site size and allowable uses, you can run numbers for multiple ideas. What types of added space appeal to a target market? More living space? Covered parking? RV parking? A workshop? Tennis courts or swimming pool? Storage shed? Community garden? Decks or patios? A gazebo? A combination card room, computer facility, or study area? A guest cottage or accessory apartment? A pet kennel? What else can you think of?

When buildable land remains scarce, figure out a way to convert unused legal capacity of a site into bigger profits. You need not target the same people for the "extra" as you do for the main buildings. If you

<blockquote>
Upgrade the use of the site.
</blockquote>

hold the property as a rental, create RV spaces or storage areas for those apartment dwellers down the block. Or if you fix and flip, accent the extra rental income as an affordability helper (cash flow generator) to homebuyers or investors.

Hidden Value in the Land   Not far from where I live, some home-owners with large lots pick up an extra $3,000 to $5,000 a year in parking fees. They rent parking spaces to people attending football games and other special events at the nearby university. Thirty cars at $15 per car for 10 events each year totals $4,500 (tax free, I suspect).

Think beyond yard space. Think how you can use that land to make money. Smart investors look for sites that offer opportunities for more intense (and more profitable) uses.

Site Quality

In addition to views (pleasant or unpleasant), the quality of a site includes these features:

◆ Topography
◆ Soil condition (building capacity and percolation)
◆ Landscaping

> **Site value relates to quality as well as size.**

Topography   I owned a property that sat slightly below grade. After a hard rain, water flowed into the garage. Topography will affect the slope and positioning of the driveway (ingress/egress). Even moderate inclines can make navigation up or down difficult during snow and ice storms. Topography also can increase construction costs and expose a site to greater risk from mudslide or earthquake.

As an advantage, a downward sloping lot often opens up opportunities for finishing off or enhancing the lower level of a house. As with every feature of a property, thoughtfully anticipate both the problems and possibilities that site topography might play into.

Soil Condition   Would you like to grow a lush yard of grass? Would your buyers or tenants like to harvest vegetables from a garden? What types of flowers and shrubs do you intend to plant? Amazingly, people always notice the quality of the yard and landscaping, but few realize that the composition of the soil can enhance or frustrate a green thumb.

The composition of the soil also can create foundation problems. For example, soil with a high content of clay tends to expand and contract. Houses built improperly on clay can split apart. When a property lacks city water and sewage disposal, verify sufficient water to sink a well and percolation tests to determine whether the soil will safely diffuse waste.

Landscaping Here's where you can really add value to a property. People love a manicured lawn, flower-lined walkways, mulched shrubs, and flower gardens. With landscaping, you can turn an ugly-duckling house into a showcase property. With landscaping you can create privacy, manufacture a gorgeous view looking out from inside the house, or eliminate an ugly view. Especially if you're looking at a three- to five-year holding period (or longer), put in those small plants, shrubs, and hedges now. When you sell, you can easily earn a payback of 10:1.

The rear boundary of one of my properties is lined with a row of hedges 12 to 16 feet tall. Since this home's major living areas and master bedroom include large expanses of glass and windows that look out to the back, these hedges (and other landscaping) create both privacy and pleasant views. In contrast, the views from the house of a nearby property owner also are oriented toward the backyard rather than the street, but even though that house is more than 40 years old, no one ever planted a rear hedgerow or otherwise landscaped the backyard. As a result, each day these homeowners gaze out at a barren yard, and each evening as they turn on the lights, they must draw their blinds. Otherwise, their rear yard neighbors can see directly into their house—for they, too, have never invested in privacy fencing or landscaping. In contrast to these homes, I am sure that the privacy/view advantage of my property boosts its value by $25,000 and adds $50 to $100 a month to its rental income.

> **Think long term. Add value-enhancing plants and trees now.**

To create value with landscaping, spruce up the yard in these ways:

◆ Remove all litter and debris from the yard and streetscape.
◆ Prune, cut back, or remove all out-of-control or straggly bushes.
◆ Edge walks and driveways. Apply weed killer to stop growth between the cracks.
◆ Trim unsightly trees and remove dead branches.
◆ Fertilize the grass and plant or create some type of attractive ground cover to eliminate those bare spots in the yard.

Remember, the yard of a property helps create (or destroy) that curb appeal.

Fences, Driveway, and Sidewalks

Assess the quality of the property's fences, driveway, sidewalks, patios, lampposts, and mailbox. After you fix up a property, none of these site features should show disrepair. Get rid of those driveway oil stains; patch cracks; and paint the lamppost, clean its light fixture, and replace broken glass. If a public sidewalk crosses the property, call the city to request (insist on) needed maintenance. Invest $35 to buy a premium mailbox. No single small expense so clearly states pride of property.

> **Displeasing site features destroy curb appeal.**

For reasons of aesthetics, privacy, and security, quality fences can really lift the value of a property—especially when combined with well-selected, eye-pleasing landscaping. Just as certainly, a rusted, rotted, or half-falling-down fence signals that the property suffers poor maintenance.

Curb Appeal: Attending to the Details

As a buyer-fixer, I love to find properties with rundown yards, landscaping, and fencing. Taken together—even more than the exterior of the property itself—these deteriorated features lock a negative impression into the minds of most buyers. These negatives heavily discount the property's curb appeal and its market value. Among all of the improvements that you can make to a property, creating dazzling curb (and backyard) appeal will pay back your investment many times over. But you must attend to details.

The Well-Dressed Man or Woman Think of the well-dressed man or woman. Both achieve that spectacular look by paying attention to a dozen or more details. Hair, makeup, jewelry, color, style, fit, freshly cleaned and pressed—everything works together. Now, place a stain on a blouse or tie and what do you get? A negative impression—that's what people remember.

Achieve Dazzling Curb Appeal Unless you're creatively gifted, *great* ideas to improve the site may not come easily. They don't come easily to me. I rank high among the artistically challenged. Here's how I overcame this obstacle.

> **Lack artistic flair? Look for model properties you can copy.**

I carry a camera in the glovebox of my car. When I spot a house and yard that display eye-catching features, I snap a picture. Over time, I've put together a large collection of photos. Then, as I figure out how to improve a fixer property, I pull out some of these photos and compare the features of model properties with the fixer property I'm improving. This method always brings forth a rush of value-creating ideas. Try it; you'll like it.

You don't need to rely on your own snapshots. Dozens of "house and home" books and magazines fill the shelves of bookstores and supermarkets. I've bought stacks of these publications. Such articles and photos will sharpen your creative thinking and aesthetic sensibilities.

The Outside of the Property

After you thoroughly inspect a site, inspect the exterior of the property. You're about to climb into the ring for the main event. To evaluate the exterior and generate ideas, focus on four criteria:

1. Appearance
2. Condition
3. Building materials and maintenance expense
4. Site placement (how the house is oriented on the site)

Appearance

Stand back from the property 50 to 100 feet. Place the building in perspective with the site and with other properties in the neighborhood. Does it fit in? Is it too large or too small? Does the architectural style give the house an appealing uniqueness? Or is it a boring box design with no windows on either side? Are there a half-dozen other houses in the neighborhood that show a similar (or even cookie-cutter) design?

> **View the property from across the street. Gain perspective.**

> **A few loss-leader repairs can pay off by bolstering the total impact of the property.**

The Roof   Pay attention to the roof. Is it discolored? Are leaves piling up? Are plants growing on the roof or out of the gutters? Roofs scare most buyers because they're costly to replace. Clean it up such that it shows as little wear as possible.

If your remedial efforts can't improve the appearance—and you plan to quickly flip the property—go ahead and replace the roof. As Bob Bruss points out, a new roof probably won't give you a dollar-for-dollar payback, but it will enhance the home's marketability.

Here's how Bruss describes the sound principle behind this advice:

Last week I was in Walgreens where they had a special on 24 cans of Coors beer for $11. That's a *very* good bargain! When I asked the manager how he can make any profit at that price, he claimed that was his cost for the beer. But, as he looked at my full shopping cart of other more profitable items which I bought during the same visit, he pointed to them and said, "That's where we make our profits." The same principle applies to fixer-upper houses. Some items you install won't add to the value of the house yet enable you to sell or rent the house at an overall profit.

To illustrate, at a house I am remodeling I am installing a new roof even though (1) it won't add any market value to the house and (2) the old roof doesn't leak—yet! Why am I so foolish? *That roof is like Walgreens' loss-leader beer special.* I know from experience one of the first questions prospective home buyers ask is "How old is the roof?" If they are reassured the roof is brand new, that makes the sale possible. But if they are told "It doesn't leak but is about 15 years old" that creates a negative rather than a positive buying situation. If your fixer-upper house obviously needs some work, such as a new roof, but you know that item won't be profitable, do it anyway if it will be a big incentive for the buyer to buy.

I must hasten to add it doesn't pay to acquire houses which need lots of unprofitable work. Examples of costly, unprofitable but usually necessary work include new roof, foundation repairs or replacement, replumbing, rewiring, and a new furnace or air conditioning system. When you inspect a fixer-upper house which needs all or most of these unprofitable improvements, just walk away *unless* you can get a very low purchase price and extremely attractive purchase terms.[1]

Bruss is right. A new roof can prove to be your most profitable loss leader. But if you only sell loss leaders, you will go broke.

Sharpen the Appeal   Can you imagine ways to enhance the property's value with window shutters, flowerboxes, a dramatic front door and

---

[1]Quoted from the Robert Bruss Real Estate Newsletter, #92215.

entryway, new or additional windows, fresh paint, a contrasting color for trim, or accenting the design with architectural details? How well does (or could) the property's exterior distinguish it from other comparably priced properties? Do you rate its appeal as great, so-so, or awful? List possibilities for profitable improvements.

Start poring over your photo collection. Look for features that set a property apart from its competitors. Use features that wow a target market.

Exterior Condition: The Professional Inspection

To avoid profit-draining loss-leader repairs, hire a professional property inspector to detect potential problems. Generally, you won't order a formal report until you sign an offer that includes an inspection contingency clause. Prior to that step, perform a preprofessional inspection. Such an exam of the exterior (and interior) serves three purposes:

1. *Negotiate more persuasively.* To achieve your price and terms, justify your offer. The seller says, "What!? You're offering me $315,000!? The house three doors down sold two months ago for $345,000." "Yes," you respond. "But that house was in near-perfect condition. As we discussed, this property is going to need. . . ."

2. *Weed out losers.* When your preinspection identifies problems, yet the seller won't accept concessions (price, terms), stop wasting time. Say *sayonara*. Move on to your next possibility.

3. *Better understand the property.* When you bring a professional inspector in, don't settle for an inspection. Get educated. Ask detailed questions. Use notes from your personal inspection to quiz the pro. Learn to spot problems and understand their causes, remedial alternatives, and, most importantly, the best cost-effective means to prevent (or delay) future trouble.

Materials and Maintenance

Each area of the country uses its own types of construction materials that are popular and effective for that locale. Wood, brick, brick veneer, adobe, concrete block, stucco, and steel are possibilities. In addition, some houses are built on a pier-and-beam foundation; others sit on concrete slabs. Windows and roofs differ, too. Crank-style aluminum awning windows are popular in some warmer climates but are seldom found up north. In California, you see tile roofs; in Maine, that type of roof is rare.

Evaluate the Quality of Construction and Building Materials Regardless of the specific types of construction materials used in your area, they vary widely in costs, function, and desirability. Before buying, talk to knowledgeable builders, contractors, or building supply companies. Learn the differences between high-end, mid-range, and low-cost building materials. Talk with anyone you know who has recently built a new house. They've probably spent months shopping for materials. To compare houses effectively, move beyond appearance. Savvy investors don't judge the quality of a house merely by its paint job.

Maintenance: Time, Effort, and Costs Apart from the quality of construction materials, consider how much time, effort, and money it's going to cost to maintain the house. Growing up, I recall that every three or four years we had to scrape peeling paint with a wire brush to prepare our home for its next coat of paint. Now, today's durable paints, stains, and materials can last 10 years or longer.

> **Always use low-maintenance materials—even when they cost more.**

When you repair or renovate, go with low- or no-maintenance improvements, even if they cost more. Neither you, your buyers, nor your tenants want to fool around with maintenance. Low- or no-maintenance features sell (rent) properties.

For lower- to moderate-priced properties, I favor vinyl siding and eaves. In the South, I like concrete block. Slap on a coat of paint every 10 to 20 years and that's it for most exterior maintenance. As to gutters, old-timers love them. I hate them. The best way to deal with rusty, leaf-filled gutters is rip them off and don't replace them. Place a rain diverter on the roof above the front porch or above other exterior entryways.

As I have mentioned, I lack the talent, inclination, and time to personally take on the chores of property repair and property maintenance. With today's materials, that distaste erects no barriers to owning small investment properties.

Site Placement

When you look at a house from the outside, note how the building is situated on the site. Are the windows positioned to bring in beacons of natural light? How about privacy from neighbors? Can residents sunbathe in the backyard without prying eyes to invade their privacy? Are the sleeping areas of the house protected from street noise? How will prevailing winter winds (or summer breezes) strike the house? How will these affect resident comfort and energy bills? In North America, a southern exposure with large windows will bring in the winter sunshine and reduce heating costs.

> **Site placement affects views, privacy, and energy efficiency.**

Does the site placement conform to the standards of *feng shui*? If your target market of buyers or tenants includes Asians, get up to speed on *feng shui* by reading one of many books published on the topic. In California, some homebuilders and renovators specifically design their houses to conform to *feng shui* principles to give their properties a competitive edge with Asian buyers.

After you thoroughly evaluate the site and the exterior of the property, next inspect the interior for problems and possibilities.

CHAPTER 6

Enhance the Interior

As you inspect the inside of a property, balance the critical with the entrepreneurial. Itemize what's wrong to help you negotiate better price and terms. Detail what's right to help you turn property potential into moneymaking improvements.

Question Square-Footage Figures

Real estate agents and appraisers value home values with price per-square-foot figures. (A 1,500-square-foot house listed at $300,000 would

> **Do not count all square footage equally.**

show a price of $200 per square foot.) The agent or the seller of a property might say something like, "We got a property bargain priced at just $175 per square foot. Nothing else in the neighborhood has sold for anything under $200 per square foot."

It sounds good so far. But before you bite, check the facts.

Watch Out for Errors of Measurement

Appraisers, sales agents, sellers, and property tax assessors mismeasure properties all the time. In fact, sellers or realty agents often pull their square-footage figures from property tax records. Yet in many areas of the country, property tax records are notoriously inaccurate. That's one reason why the fine print on the Realtor's property description flyers says, "Data believed to be from reliable sources, but not warranted."

> **Verify who has measured what.**

Recently, an appraiser reported the square footage of one of my properties at 1,370 square feet, when it actually comes close to 1,750 square feet. The property tax records of one house I owned showed 2,460 square feet. But the house actually totaled over 3,200 square feet because the tax assessor had never adjusted his figures to reflect an 800-square-foot addition.

Of course, errors also may plague the reported square footages of comp properties. The comp price per square foot could exceed or fall below the figures quoted.

All Space Doesn't Count Equally

The square footage of an attic that's been converted into a spare bedroom isn't worth as much as the square footage of the main house. A finished basement of 800 square feet doesn't equal an 800-square-foot second story that's fully integrated into the house. Don't compare houses or apartment units only in size; compare the quality and livability of the finished space.

Remember this point not only when you're bidding on a property but when you make improvements. Amateur renovators add space through bastardized conversions that feature low ceilings, rooms without windows, weird hallways, and no ductwork for heat or air conditioning. To enhance the value of a property, integrate the new space within the existing building such that it harmonizes. Ill-designed conversions and additions diminish value and turn off potential buyers and tenants.

> **Avoid bastardized conversions and remodelings.**

Nevertheless, when you come upon those bastardized conversions and additions, put on your rose-colored glasses. Can you remedy the oddball appearance? Can you redesign and enhance functional utility? I often find that by investing a few thousand dollars along with some creative insights, I can transform awkward space arrangements into open, smoothly flowing areas.

Make Sure All Like Space Does Count Equally

Some sellers count all space with a roof over it. Others count only the basic living areas. The sellers of one house may describe its size as 1,980 square feet and include in that square-footage figure a garage that's now a den conversion. An owner of a similar home may describe that house as 1,600 square feet and simply footnote a similarly converted makeshift den as an extra, but not include its size in the square footage quoted for the house.

In appraising the market value of one of my properties, the appraiser listed a comp property at a size of 2,200 square feet. Yet, I had visited that property during an open house when it was available for sale. I knew that its square footage didn't come close to the size the appraiser had reported.

What accounted for the difference? The appraiser believed that the comp property's garage had been converted to living space because the property owners had constructed one of those awning-type carports over the driveway. The appraiser carelessly counted the comp house garage as living area (when in fact it was being used as storage for a home business), whereas he counted the garage of my property as a garage. Like spaces weren't counted equally.

> **Appraisers follow slipshod practices.**

Appraisers Seldom Inspect Comp Houses
How could the appraiser make this mistake? Easy. Appraisers seldom inspect their comp houses. They'll drive by and snap several photos. But they won't

walk the property or go inside. During boom housing markets (sales and refis), appraisers try to complete 8 to 12 appraisal assignments a day. At that breakneck pace, no appraiser takes the time to weigh and consider. The superficial and impressionistic kicks aside care and reason.

Fixer Profits Require Detailed and Accurate Property Inspections and Comparisons   Appraisers, sales agents, sellers, and even investors accept and repeat inappropriate price-per-square-foot figures. It's such a widely quoted rule-of-thumb that buyers overlook its complexity and inconsistencies. Avoid this casual approach. When someone quotes you a price-per-square-foot number, question its accuracy and applicability.

To earn flip and fix profits, you must (1) accurately value a property in its as-is condition; and (2) accurately estimate the minimum (reasonable) improved value (MIV). When employed carefully, square footage comparisons give you a good idea of relative home values in a neighborhood. Used naively, they mislead you into believing that you've landed a bargain when you've actually overpaid. Or, you could overestimate the value of that basement or attic conversion you're planning. Your payback would fall short of your profit goals.

I routinely use price-per-square-foot figures, but only after I've adjusted them for quality, consistency, and accuracy. How do you gain this ability? Go to open houses. Inspect the neighborhood properties that come up for sale. Judge the size, quality, and condition of these houses. Track selling prices. Then when a seller, realty agent, or appraiser throws out a per-square-foot figure, you'll know whether that figure makes sense.

> **Quality adjust all per-square-foot value estimates.**

Floor Plan: Does the Layout of the Property Work?

Once you have moved beyond the size of a house, evaluate its floor plan. Does the layout offer convenience and privacy? Does it work effectively and efficiently?

When you approach the entry of the house, do you climb steep steps? Is there a covered porch area so visitors can avoid standing in the rain or snow while waiting for someone in the house to answer their knock? If the entrance lies below grade, does it appear that water may build up in the entrance area? As you walk in the front door, notice whether you're dropped immediately into a living area or does the house include a foyer? Is there a coat closet nearby? Relative to the main entrance, where is the kitchen located? Can you walk from the entry door to other rooms of the house without passing through a third room? How are the location and size of bedrooms, baths, and closets?

Livability

Now, imagine people living in the unit. Where will their kids play—both indoors and outdoors? Will the parents be able to keep an eye on them? Does the house have a "Grand Central Station" living room? Or is it pleasantly isolated from other house activity areas?

> **Square footage doesn't mean livability.**

Go into the kitchen. How long does it take the faucet to draw hot water? For purposes of work efficiency, can you step conveniently between the refrigerator, oven, stovetop, and sink? Do you see adequate counter and cabinet space? Is there an eat-in kitchen area that separates the family members who are eating from those who are working (preparing meals, cleaning up)? Can you easily access the kitchen from the garage or carport? Can you conveniently enter the kitchen from the parking area while carrying several bags of groceries?

On this tour to evaluate floor plan, make back-and-forth trips throughout the house as if you were living there. Perhaps the long walk from the kitchen to the master bedroom wouldn't faze an investor on a quick walkthrough. But how would you like to make that trip a dozen times a day or more? Would it prove tiresome? Where's the laundry located? Is the floor plan open or closed? Does the house live to the front or the rear? Detail your observations. Think target market.

Target Market

Will the layout appeal to your target market? Alternatively, can you think of certain types of buyers or tenants who would find the floor plan especially appealing? For example, residents with small children typically prefer to have the master bedroom close to the kids' bedrooms. Seniors typically prefer single-story houses with few steps. Rental roommates generally like separate privacy areas, especially split floor plans. How about a home office? Is there a large, private room that could serve the person who works at home?

> **Imagine people living in the house.**

Some investors focus on the price, physical condition, and appearance of a property and fail to imagine its livability. In contrast, think like buyers (or tenants). As they move through the house, they begin to visualize people, activities, and furniture in various rooms and areas. They ask themselves and imagine:

- Where will the kids play, sleep, and entertain friends?
- Where will we place our furniture?
- Where will we eat family dinners?
- How conveniently can we work in the kitchen?
- Where's a good place for the workshop?
- Does the kitchen include enough cabinets and storage space?
- Where will we entertain our friends?
- Will we have enough room for guests when they visit?
- Will we have enough closet space?
- Will members of the household be able to enjoy privacy and quiet zones?

> **Anticipate the needs and wants of your buyers and tenants.**

As you get to know your target market, anticipate their concerns and needs. Understand what features light up their eyes and what features close their minds to the property. To learn these features, talk with potential buyers (tenants), visit open houses, tour model new homes, confer with real estate agents, and through any and all other methods of discovery that you can think of.

Savvy renovators don't just "fix and repair ugly houses." More importantly, through their property improvements, they make living easier for their buyers and tenants.

Rightsize Rooms and Room Counts Some houses and apartments include bedrooms no larger than a closet and bathrooms no larger than a phone booth. Can you figure a way to increase their size or change their use to better match buyer needs? Or could you subdivide that cavernous great room into smaller living areas? As you judge the room sizes and room counts (number of bedrooms, bathrooms, living areas, kitchens, home office) within a house, try to generate ideas about how you could employ the space more effectively.

Ill-Designed Houses Dominate the Market Many older and even newer houses were ill designed at the time they were built. Others were okay for the 1930s, 1940s, or 1950s, but no longer reflect modern tastes. I like to find houses with those old-fashioned closed floor plans (each room separate and distinct from all others) and open them up with a living space that flows through the kitchen, dining, and living areas.

> **Modernize a floor plan for big profits.**

Make the Kitchen Work Better When kitchens are too large, I tighten up the work triangle and add either a small office/bill-paying type of workstation or an eat-in area if none previously existed. Or maybe I'll do both. A center island with a counter overhang and stools tucked underneath can serve double duty as a food preparation area and an informal sit-down, in-kitchen eating area. And you can still create a household office area.

Closets and Bedrooms In some older houses, the bedrooms are large, but the closets won't hold much more than a navy trunk. When you find a house that fits this description, do as I have done. Trade two feet of bedroom for a wall-length closet. If you buy a house with one or two small bedrooms, you could install a Murphy bed. This tactic will permit the residents of the house to make more effective use of the floor space. You could also build in a loft bed, which will free up floor space.

Install Pocket Doors   Sometimes the way a door swings can chew up livable space. I like to put in pocket doors if the studs permit. These can work well to make better use of the off-bedroom bath. Because pocket doors cost more to install, few people use them. But many buyers consider pocket doors a special touch. Also, you can add space to a room by reversing the swing of an existing door.

Increase Storage Areas   You can think about storage space in at least three ways:

1.   Bring dead space to life.
2.   Rightsize existing storage space.
3.   Create new space.

Bring Dead Space to Life.   Let me illustrate with what seems trivial, but in fact always creates a lasting favorable impression. Look in the cabinet under your kitchen sink. You will see a small gap between the front panel of the cabinet above the door and the sink. In other words, dead space. How might you use that space? Install a small pull-down compartment to stow away soap, sponge, and Brillo pad—no more sink clutter. When I show off this little innovation to other people, I always get a "Wow, isn't that neat" response.

> **Everyone wants more storage. Give it to them.**

Okay, I admit it's trivial. But it illustrates the point. All houses include generous amounts of large and small dead spaces that with creativity you can bring to life:

◆ Under stairs and stairwells
◆ On the tops of kitchen cabinets
◆ Under porches
◆ Dead-end cabinets

♦ Walls suitable for shelving
♦ Interior access to an under-the-house crawl space
♦ Recessed storage between studs (as with an in-wall medicine chest)
♦ Kitchen hanging bars for pots and pans

Rightsize Existing Storage Space   My favorite examples to illustrate this point come from the California Closet Company (CCC). As this innovative firm has proven, you can double (or triple) your storage capacity without adding even one square inch of new space. Simply reorganize and redesign the raw space that already exists. Although founded as a closet company, CCC now redesigns garages, offices, workshops, and kitchens. Put these same organizing principles to work and you'll truly enhance the appeal of your properties.

> **Take a cue from the California Closet Company.**

Create New Space   My father ran out of space in his garage to store all of his lawn and garden equipment. But through creative design, he added about 100 square feet of space to the end of the garage for a cost of just $1,000—a mere $10 per square foot. Plus, because much of the "shed" is glass with a southern exposure, he's able to also use it as a makeshift greenhouse to hang his tomato plants and get a head start on the Indiana growing season.

As you evaluate properties, look for dead spaces and functionally deficient existing storage areas. But if these improvements still don't wow your buyers, build new space—with multiple purposes.

Aesthetics: How Does the Property Look, Feel, and Sound?

"I was once in a house," recalls real estate appraiser Dodge Woodson, "that made me feel as if there should have been a coffin sitting in the living room. The drapes were dark and heavy—a ghastly green that gave

> **Homes sell with emotional appeal.**

me an eerie feeling. I don't spook easily, and I'm used to seeing a lot of houses in a lot of different conditions, but this house made me uncomfortable. If I had been a prospective buyer, I would not have been able to focus on anything but the drapes."

Woodson's reaction to this house with the eerie dark-green drapes wouldn't have surprised Professor Mary Jasmosli of George Washington University. Jasmosli has developed an expertise she calls *environmental sensitivity*. Through her research she has found that people react emotionally to the interiors (and exteriors) of homes in ways that they themselves can neither explain nor understand. "Home features such as number of windows, window treatments, color schemes, views, placement of walls and doorways, room size, ceiling height, and amount of light all hold special meaning," reports Jasmosli.

Now, we're turning to Dodge Woodson. "The next time I entered that house, I couldn't believe the difference," he remarks. "The owners had replaced the dark-green drapes with flowing white window treatments. . . . Not only was the house pretty, it appeared much larger. . . . I noticed features that I had never seen before. The house was alive with light. This experience convinced me of the power that window treatments have."

Create Emotional Appeal

It's not just window treatments that can change the emotional appeal of a home. You can dramatically improve the look and feel of any home. Change, replace, or remove any of its negatives. If you look at a house that doesn't generate the warmth, brightness, or romance you think your buyers or tenants would pay extra for, don't rush to get back in your car. Linger. Isolate the sources of your discomfort. Mull over ideas. How would the house (or apartment units) look, feel, sound, or smell if you:

- ◆ Put in skylights.
- ◆ Remove a wall.
- ◆ Eliminate the litter box and pet odors.

◆ Replace the worn, ugly carpeting.

◆ Increase the size or number of windows or add brighter, more modern window treatments.

◆ Create a view with a flower garden or arrangement of plants, shrubs, or hedges.

◆ Paint and wallpaper with different colors and textures.

◆ Install new cabinets or appliances.

◆ Pull out that dropped-ceiling acoustical tile and create a vaulted ceiling.

◆ Soundproof the home with insulated windows, shrubs, or an earth berm.

Put your imagination to work. With good ideas you can transform any property, making it more comfortable, appealing, and valuable. In some cases, emotional appeal will even trump function and floor plan.

> **Strong emotional appeal often overwhelms cool-headed negatives.**

In buying one of my previous homes, I was so smitten with its wooded views, expansive windows, beamed ceilings, hardwood floors, skylights, and Jacuzzi in the master bathroom, I didn't think carefully about floor plan, internal traffic patterns, and functional efficiency. After moving in, I recognized flaws in the home's design and function. The master bedroom was located directly above the den, and sounds from the television came right up; the water heater lacked enough capacity to fill the Jacuzzi; and access to the kitchen from the garage was quite cumbersome for carrying in bags of groceries. (I might add that this house was only three years old!)

Check Noise Levels

Noise creates a potential problem within households. Will sound from a television or stereo carry into other rooms? Bring along a portable radio on your house inspections. Place it in various rooms. Turn up the volume. Are the walls reasonably soundproof? Families and roommate tenants want privacy and quiet. If your property fails to offer these essentials, your property will lose its appeal.

Just as important, will residents hear neighbors or neighborhood noise from inside the house? Again, people pay for quiet. They discount for noise.

Although potential neighbors and neighborhood noise are especially important to note in townhouses and condominiums, single-family developments are no strangers to loud stereos, barking dogs, and Indy 500 engine revving. Does the drum corps of the nearby high school practice outside three or four hours a day? When possible, visit the property during periods of high traffic or peak noise. Don't assume that a neighborhood offers peace and quiet. Verify.

> **Buyers (renters) pay premiums for quiet.**

Seek written disclosures from the sellers. Talk with neighbors. Determine whether anyone has tried to enforce quiet by complaining to city government or the homeowners association, or by filing a nuisance suit. If you buy the property, could you pursue these remedies? Could the house, itself, incorporate more features to reduce noise that emanates from either the outside or the inside of the house? When you suppress noise, you create value.

Clean Thoroughly

Perhaps more than any other common problem, dirt turns buyers (and tenants) off. Dirty windows; accumulated dirt and debris on porches, patios, and entryways; and even old and dirty doormats seem to build a wall of emotional resistance. Dirt signals that a house has not been well cared for. Most tenants and buyers steer clear of dirty properties.

> **Clean pays back many times over.**

Now, imagine the home's appeal if it were given a top-to-bottom cleaning. Because houses with dirty exteriors frequently have unkempt yards, you may have to picture the home as if the grass were neatly cut, the shrubs trimmed, and the flowers blooming. Close your eyes. Now what does the house look like?

In their idea-generating book, *Dress Your House for Success* (Three Rivers Press, 1997, pp. 73–74), Martha Webb and Sarah Zackhem write:

> The uncomfortable feeling an of unclean house causes apprehension, and the buyer will start to disengage . . . when she finds accumulated dust, dirt, grime, mildew, or soap scum, she mentally disengages because she's slightly embarrassed of what else she might find. For the rest of the house tour, she will become remote, hesitant, and will proceed with a detached attitude. And guaranteed, when later she thinks of your house—if she thinks of it at all—she will most remember the dirt.

After this introduction, Webb and Zackhem continue with eight pages of specific cleaning details. When they say clean, they mean *clean.*

- Spotless windows and mirrors.
- High-luster interior wood.
- Crumbless kitchen drawers and cabinets.
- Fresh paint wherever walls or other painted surfaces refuse to give up their previous scuffs and marks.
- No dust or dead insects inside light fixtures.
- No collected dirt or dust in corners or along baseboards.
- Scrub down to perfection all faucets, sinks, showers, toilets, and bathtubs.
- Replace or refinish wherever stains persist.

Their list goes on. But you see their point. Clean means perfection. To achieve this goal, here's a trick that I've used. Hire an 8- or 10-year-old. Tell the child that you will pay him or her five dollars base pay to seek out flaws in your house preparation plus a dollar for each flaw discovered. After cleaning inside and out, you still need fresh eyes to give the house another detailed inspection. You never get a second chance to create a stunning first impression.

Condition: How Much Time, Effort, and Money Will the Property Require?

Before you close on a property, hire a professional to inspect it. Place an inspection contingency in your written offer to the sellers. Depending on what the inspector turns up, you can move forward with your purchase, renegotiate price and repair credits, or withdraw from the agreement. Before you hire a professional, though, closely check the condition of the property yourself.

First, get an idea about a property's condition so that you can compare various properties to each other. Second, use shortcomings to persuade sellers to concede a lower price, better terms, or an escrow credit for repairs. Third, weed out some properties because they require too many money-losing repairs and replacements (the wrong things are wrong).

> **Properties that need repairs frighten many buyers.**

For an interior preprofessional inspection, here are six items to evaluate: (1) plumbing; (2) heating, ventilating, and air conditioning; (3) electrical; (4) ceilings, walls, and floors; (5) appearance and floor plan; and (6) quality of materials.

1. *Plumbing.* To check the condition of the plumbing, first test the water pressure. Turn on a couple of baths or showers, then flush the toilets. What happens? Is the water pressure sufficient to maintain the water flows? Check all the water faucets for drips. Determine whether the water heater is large enough to allow all members of a household to take hot showers when everybody is trying to get ready at the same time. Inspect all the pipes and shutoff valves under sinks and cabinets. Is there any sign of leaking, rust, or corrosion? If the house has a basement or accessible crawl space, inspect the plumbing from that vantage point. What type of piping has been used—plastic, copper, galvanized steel, lead, or something else? Each of these materials has its own advantages and disadvantages, installation procedures, and

building code standards. Discuss these points with a professional inspector.

2. *Heating, ventilating, and air conditioning (HVAC).* Depending on the season of the year, you may not be able to adequately test the HVAC system of a house. But, at least note the placement and size of the duct vents. Do any rooms lack outlets? Are the vents positioned to evenly and efficiently distribute heat throughout a house? If the house (or specific rooms) lacks central heat or air (e.g., it has floor furnaces, wall furnaces, or window heat and air units), residents may experience hot and cool spots throughout the house. Because most HVAC equipment has a limited life, ask the ages of various components. An age of more than 8 or 10 years may point to coming problems. (Though, one house I own was built in 1967 and its original GE five-ton central air system—heat is gas—still works well.)

3. *Electrical.* As with plumbing and HVAC systems, judge the condition of an electrical system by how well it will serve the household needs and whether it meets modern standards of performance and safety. Reserve this latter question for your expert. But you can evaluate the home's amperage (60, 100, or 200) and voltage (115 or 230); whether it has circuit breakers or an old-fashioned fuse box; and the number, location, and convenience of electrical outlets, switches, and built-in light fixtures.

4. *Ceilings, walls, and floors.* As you walk through a house, examine the ceilings, walls, floors, and floor coverings. Note their condition, but also note any related problems. Water stains may indicate roof or plumbing leaks. Cracks may point to foundation problems. Check floors to see whether they are level. Would a marble placed in the center of the room roll swiftly to one side or the other? Don't feel as if you're out of line to pull back rugs, peek behind pictures, and look under furniture. More than a few sellers have been known to selectively place wall hangings, rugs, and furniture to hide stains, cracks, or other defects. I once pulled back a room-sized Oriental rug and discovered the underlying floor was particleboard—though hardwood flooring showed around the outside edges of the rug.

5. *Appearance and floor plan.* A property may not *require* any redecorating, repairs, or remodeling. Yet, it still may not look good. If that shag carpeting or closed-in kitchen doesn't meet contemporary tastes and preferences, you must spend some time and money to bring the house up to higher standards. But if you redecorate or remodel simply to suit your own preferences (as opposed to those of your buyers or tenants), you may not make money from your improvements. If you own the house for the long term or rank tenant satisfaction above profit, then change the property to match your tastes. Just realize the difference between profitable and personal improvements. (Of course, in this instance you might profit from quicker renting, lower vacancies, and less tenant turnover.)

6. *Quality of materials.* Note the quality of the materials used throughout the property's interior. The cost of carpeting may range from $10 per square yard up to $100 or more. Some interior flat-paneled, hollow-core doors sell for $15 to $25 each. Other doors, solid wood, stained, and decorative paneled, can cost upward of $500 each. You can buy a set of kitchen cabinets for $1,500 or $150,000. Low-grade vinyl floor coverings run $5 per square yard. Top-of-the-line can cost $25 per square yard or more.

You'll find similar differences in quality and costs for light fixtures, wood paneling, paints, wallpapers, sinks, bathtubs, faucets, and nearly all other interior building materials. Although cost seldom correlates one-to-one with value, buyers do expect to pay something extra for a property that includes better-grade materials. Just evaluate with caution. Study buyer preferences. Price realistically. You'll earn a good return on your improvement dollars.

Legal Compliance

As you go through a property, look for illegal or nonconforming use. Ask the sellers for written disclosures. Tell your professional inspector

<table>
<tr><td>

Know the codes. Watch for violations.

</td><td>

to alert you to any areas of noncompliance that he spots. Although inspectors don't specifically give legal opinions, most will voice their concerns—especially if the violations affect health or safety. If your compliance discovery points to code infrac-tions, confirm your suspicions with the city regu-

</td></tr>
</table>

lators. Determine whether code enforcers think the problem major, minor, or of no concern.

(I remind you to verify that your planned work will conform to code. Spend only for permitted and compliant repairs or improvements.)

Estimate Costs of Repairs and Improvements

As a neophyte fixer, you will rely on experts for your cost estimates. But be forewarned. You need to educate yourself as you go along.

I secured bids from a recommended plumbing contractor to completely replumb a house. When the house was built, 50 years ago, the pipes were laid in the concrete slab foundation but were now springing leaks. Rather than suffer repeated repairs, I decided to replace. This contractor bid $5,500 and explained how running new pipes would require large amounts of cutting through walls and ceilings.

I know little about the fine points of plumbing, but I could see that this estimate of costs and plan of repair did not make sense. It was time for a second opinion.

The Second Opinion   The next contractor who bid gave an estimate of $2,800 (same quality of materials). He said that his workmen could thread the new pipe through just a few small exterior wall cuts and one small cut through a closet wall. After getting one more bid ($3,300), I awarded the job to the "second opinion" contractor. True to his word, his firm completed the job as promised, on time, and for the amount bid.

(Note: When you replumb a house built on concrete slab, you run the new pipe around the exterior of the house. However, when you

> **Contractors manage and design their work much differently.**

repair slab pipe, you must jackhammer the concrete in the area where you think you hear or feel the pipe leaking.)

Learn by Doing   How did I sense that the first cost estimate and plan of repair was way out of line? Because I always listen closely and try to follow the reasoning.

Even though someone else wears the mantle of *expert*, exercise your critical faculties. Whenever you secure estimates, obtain multiple bids. Ask contractors to explain their methods and plan of completion. Consult personnel at lumberyards, hardware stores, and home supply companies. Talk with property owners who have completed similar work. Learn to distinguish reasonable from unreasonable estimates of costs and work plans.

> **Learn from experts. Don't let them bamboozle you.**

Published Cost Estimates   Often you see estimates of repair and improvement costs published in magazine articles and books. Read these with casual interest, but your actual costs will undoubtedly differ.

Costs vary too much to apply universally. As with my plumbing contractors, the highest estimate more than doubled the lowest estimate. (Because plumbers do not repair the "mess" they make cutting through tile, walls, or ceilings, you must pay someone else to restore what the plumber damaged.) Estimates vary by the time of the year, the area of the country, the job backlog of the contractor, and the detailed repairs that the job will require—some of which may not be known until the job begins. (That's why you add an *oops* factor to your cost estimates.)

> **Avoid paying retail.**

Search Out Bargain-Priced Materials   You may be able to buy excellent quality used items. I once bought a complete high-quality kitchen—I mean the entire kitchen stripped to bare walls—from some wealthy homeowners who did not like the color of the kitchen in the house they had just bought. They decided to tear out the old and install another kitchen that met their tastes. You can sometimes gain from the extravagant waste of other property owners.

Sometimes you find great bargains in closeout sales, scratched and dented merchandise, and inventory overstocks. I sometimes talk with contractors on large commercial jobs to learn whether they're going to discard materials that I can buy cheaply. Buildings that are scheduled to be moved or torn down can also yield treasures (such as light fixtures, wood flooring, doors, wood paneling, cabinets, shelving, carpeting, or maybe even an antique Victorian claw-footed bathtub).

As a savvy, entrepreneurial renovator, search out bargain-priced contractors and materials. Forget that old saw, "You get what you pay for." When renovating, you can spend a lot for a little, or a little for a lot. Also, when you buy materials and supplies, ask merchants for contractor discounts.

Utility Bills (Energy Efficiency)

Utility bills rank as the second- or third-largest expense in the budgets of many families. During months of peak usage, utility bills of $200 to $500 a month are common. As you compare properties, find out (1) which utilities are available to a house, (2) how much they will cost each month, and (3) what you can do to reduce utility expenses. Lower utility bills mean a higher selling price or higher rents and less tenant turnover. High bills spur tenant revolts.

What Utilities Are Available?

A friend of mine owns a rental house near Lakeland, Florida. He recently complained that he had to install a new sewage-disposal drain field at the property. He expected the cost to run around $1,400. As we talked about this repair, this friend admitted that when he bought the house he hadn't even realized that its sewage-disposal system wasn't connected to the city sewer. As an inexperienced investor, he hadn't even thought to ask. Avoid similar mistakes. Before you offer to buy property, ask what utilities are available (sewage, disposal, water, electricity, natural gas, cable TV, digital high-speed cable, telephone, etc.). Many investors are surprised to learn that properties located within a city may lack one or more of the utilities that they previously had taken for granted. For investors in properties located in suburban or rural areas, the need to identify available utilities is even more pressing.

Identify Ways to Reduce Utility Bills

> **Energy efficiency pays off.**

After you check a property's utility bills (obtained from either the sellers or the utility companies), reduce these expenses. For example:

◆ Would more insulation, caulking, or storm doors and windows significantly lower the costs of heating and cooling?
◆ Has the water heater been wrapped with insulation?
◆ Can you profitably switch from higher-cost energy (electric) to lower-cost (natural gas)?
◆ Do utility companies offer incentives to make the property more efficient? In some cities, natural gas companies replace electric water heaters with gas water heaters at no charge to the owner. Utility companies give reduced rates to property owners or residents who agree to accept energy cutbacks during peak usage times. Companies perform energy audits on property at little or no cost.
◆ From time to time, the government, at the local, state, and federal levels, offers various tax credits, low-cost loans, and direct grants to property owners who upgrade to conserve energy. Are such benefits available for the properties that you compare?

Over a 10-year period, utility bill savings of just $100 a month will add up to nearly $18,000 (assuming interest compounded at 8 percent). Numbers like these give your properties a competitive edge.

Save on Property Taxes

Before you renovate, learn the ins and outs of the property tax laws that apply to the property. Each tax jurisdiction sets rules and procedures that govern how property improvements are assessed and taxed. Built-in cabinets and wall-to-wall carpeting will likely add to the assessed value of the property, whereas cabinets that do not attach permanently to the walls and carpeting that does not get tacked down may not count.

> **Lower the property taxes on a property.**

These examples illustrate the quirks that tax laws include. To find the quirks that can work to your favor, talk to the folks at the property tax assessor's office. If in learning the ins and outs you slice your tax bill by just 5 to 10 percent, you will save hundreds (perhaps thousands) of dollars over the years of ownership.

Save on Property Insurance

Facing low investment returns and high casualty losses, property insurers are raising rates, cutting back coverages, and tightening underwriting standards. Before you buy, check with several insurance agents to verify that you can obtain adequate insurance protection at an affordable price. Learn the types of improvements you can make that will get a rate break for you or your buyers. How about smoke alarms, earthquake retrofit, hurricane shutters, safety glass, burglar alarm, heavier locks, fencing, upgraded electrical system, and so forth? Thoroughly review the rating criteria the insurer will use. Then, where economical, adapt to fit the insurer's underwriting discounts.

Enhance the Safety and Security of Residents

Improvements to obtain lower insurance rates will help make the property safe and secure. Hazards of concern include:

- ◆ Environmental (lead paint, asbestos, mold, radon, improper discharge of wastes)
- ◆ Electrical fires
- ◆ Electrical shock
- ◆ Falls (bathtub, stairs)
- ◆ Sharp corners on countertops or other places that children can run into
- ◆ Insecure locks on windows
- ◆ Swimming pools
- ◆ Cracked sidewalks
- ◆ Dead trees or branches that overhang the house

> **Provide your buyers (tenants) a safe and secure property.**

Depending on the ages and household composition of your target market (as well as the neighborhood in which the property is located), an emphasis on special features that enhance safety and security might add to your value proposition. Apart, though, from your target market, safety check the property to eliminate all obvious dangers to life or limb.

Special-Purpose Uses

You may find that renovating toward some special-purpose use might secure a premium price or rental rate. Most renovators go generic. In return, they receive a generic profit. But when you renovate toward the specific needs of a bull's-eye segment of seniors, the disabled, children, home businesses, college students, or any other specialized target of customers, you favorably differentiate your product.

> **Tailor unique features of a property to a niche segment of buyers (tenants).**

To discover a profitable niche, talk with people at social service agencies, hospitals, and local colleges. Imagine the special needs of single parents, multigenerational households, hobbyists, roommates, group homes, and shelters. Stay alert to learn of property features and uses where demand runs strong and supply falls short. Run-of-the-mill renovators know how to fix up a property; entrepreneurs search for a special niche of customers. Then tailor the features of the property to fit that target market.

CHAPTER 7

Add More Living Space

You earn more money with a property when you create *quality* living space. As explained earlier, to value properties, investors, homebuyers, and sellers routinely use price per square foot. If you know that 1,300 to 1,600 square feet, three-bedroom, two-bath homes in a given neighborhood typically sell for $200 to $225 per square foot, then you can figure that a decent three-two, 1,400-square-foot house should sell for at least $260,000 and maybe top $352,000.

> **Match the features of the property to the zoning laws. More quality space adds value.**

Say that you search in a low-priced area of the country. You find a two-bedroom, one-bath, cosmetic fixer with just 1,100 square feet. Because of its rough condition and small size and room count, you buy this house for $80,000 ($72.72 per square foot). If you dress the house for success and add another bedroom and bath (300 square feet), your minimum improved value (MIV) should climb to around $140,000 ($100 per square foot). The question becomes, can you complete these improvements for less than, say, $30,000 to $35,000?

Work the Numbers

In my old hometown, these numbers look reasonable. In your area, the numbers may look too low (or too high). But the method works. Plug in the per square foot selling prices and compare them to the renovation costs that prevail in the cities and neighborhoods where you are looking. This strategy for improvement works best when you find fix-up houses that are relatively small compared to other nearby houses. It typically does not work well when you try to add living space to a house whose size already dwarfs neighboring properties (see forthcoming exceptions to this rule).

Attic, Garage, and Basement Conversions

When you shop properties, look for those with an attic, garage, or basement that you can convert to *quality* living space. I emphasize the words *quality space* because amateur remodelers often convert as cheaply as possible. Their finished spaces not only look cheap, they may lack natural light; the ceilings may hang too low; or the newly created traffic patterns or floor plans seem weird, convoluted, or garbled.

> **Add quality space, not space that looks weird.**

Renovators who design and finish their conversions to wow potential buyers (tenants) make serious money for their efforts. To earn good profits, your conversion should achieve the following objectives:

◆ Exceed needs and wants of a target market
◆ Show off pleasing aesthetics
◆ Integrate well within the overall plan and design of the property

Target Market Needs

If you renovate for personal use, it's okay to convert your basement into a rec room that mimics the look of a favorite bar or tavern. For profitable remodeling, please your target market. What highly valued quality space can you offer that competing properties lack? A dynamite home office, a study, a playroom for the kids, a workout area, a library, an entertainment center, a seductive master bedroom and bath? Look through other properties and that stack of remodeling and design magazines.

Aesthetics

Basement conversions fail when they lack windows, light, or smell badly with that damp, musty odor so common to below-ground living areas. To overcome such problems, use window wells and carve outs to bring in sunlight. To eliminate the musty smell and dampness, use high-quality sealants and fresh air ventilation. Follow similar ideas for attic and garage conversions. Once finished, these areas need to look, live, feel, and smell as good as the rest of the house. Add light, height, warmth, and color. Steer clear of cheap, four-foot-by-eight-foot paneling, acoustical tile ceilings, or indoor-outdoor carpeting. Create romance for your intended customers' home-to-be. Think pizzazz!

> **Can you make a basement seem homey?**

Integrate the Conversion into the House

When you evaluate properties for conversion, think of your work as expanding the total integrated living area of the house. The best conversions flow smoothly to and from the original living areas. Think access and flow. Merge the conversion into a natural traffic pattern.

Avoid signaling to your prospects, "Now entering a converted garage (basement or attic)." Or "Watch your head. The ceiling's a little low in here." Look for properties that are currently designed with potential for an integrated addition. A well-planned conversion will pay back two dollars (or more) for every dollar invested.

Create an Accessory Apartment

Variously called in-law suites, basement suites, garage apartments, mortgage helpers, or accessory apartments, these separate living units easily pay back their cost many times over. Depending on the city and neighborhood, an accessory apartment can bring in rents that range anywhere from $250 to $750 per month. Yet, unless you build from scratch, you can usually create a desirable unit for as little as $5,000 and certainly no more than $20,000.

> **Accessory apartments pay huge returns.**

Viewed in terms of return on investment, $10,000 in renovation costs can often generate a rental income of $4,000 to $6,000 per year. You can search for a long time and never find as much return for so little risk.

The Zoning Obstacle

Unfortunately, restrictive zoning ordinances exclude accessory apartments from many single-family neighborhoods. According to these ordinances, it's okay for two parents, four teenage kids, three SUVs, and two dogs and a cat to occupy a 2,200-square-foot, four-bedroom, three-bath house. But if the 75-year-old widow who lives next door to this all-American family wants to convert two spare bedrooms and a bath into an efficiency apartment to provide living quarters for a grad student from the local college, she's breaking the law.

Lax Standards of Enforcement Fortunately, such lawbreakers seldom get hauled to court. Except in elite communities with Dick Tracy investigators, most illegal accessory apartments fall into the "don't ask, don't tell," category. While I typically advise renovators to stay within the law, you might risk an exception in this case.

The U.S. now has 30 million single-person households. Many younger (and older) single persons need affordable housing. Many other households (including singles and seniors) need an extra source of income to help make mortgage payments or even to help pay living expenses. Accessory apartments benefit all concerned with no harm to anyone.

Request a Variance or a Change in the Law   To stay legal, request a zoning variance from the code enforcers. Although technically, accessory apartments don't qualify as a bona fide issue for variance, if the neighbors don't complain, you might prevail. Seek a change in the zoning law. Social service agencies support rules that permit accessory units. Enlist the power of numbers, as well as the power of persuasive reasoning. You might prevail.

Threaten a Lawsuit   If you don't win your appeal to reason, threaten a lawsuit. To pass constitutional scrutiny, zoning laws must not prove arbitrary. They must bear a close rational relationship to the objective sought. Wholesale bans on accessory apartments seem to violate this constitutional standard. Since families can fill up a neighborhood with kids, cars, and barking dogs, why can't Mrs. Widow or those newly married schoolteachers bring another person into their households? If the law related objectively to noise, parking, or condition of the property, then it could reasonably regulate accessory units but not prohibit them outright.

The (arguably) unconstitutional ordinances that ban accessory units are awakening some to review their laws. (Similarly, many cities are reviewing their hostile laws that govern or prohibit home offices and home businesses.)

> **No objective reasons stand against accessory apartments.**

As the U.S. society continues to age, we will experience more and more widows and widowers living alone in their too large, longtime family homes. Yet they do not want to move. We also see many hopeful first-time homebuyers who are priced out of the homes or neighborhoods where they would like to live. In each of these situations, an accessory apartment could serve to promote social as well as individual goals.

Fewer than 50 percent of U.S. households now consist of the traditional family of mother, father, and children. Given these demographic realities, the political winds blow stronger toward change. With more lobbying, maybe you won't need a lawsuit.

Technical Compliance As another alternative, closely read the fine print of the ordinance that prohibits or restricts accessory apartments. Often you can find loopholes. For example, most ordinances apply to separate, fully-contained living units that include a kitchen. But read how the law defines "kitchen." If you forego a full-size range in favor of a microwave, a countertop convection oven, or a hotplate, technically you might comply with the law.

> **Look for loopholes.**

If you do skirt the law, don't flaunt your civil disobedience. Do not construct an obvious direct entrance to the unit; set up an unsightly second or third parking space in the sideyard; or nail up a second mailbox. Stay incognito. Ask the tenant to receive all mail at a post office box. And if you convert a garage, blend the conversion into the design of the property—and get rid of that dead-end driveway look.

Other Zoning Districts The legal obstacles mentioned here apply to districts zoned single family.[1] If you buy a property that's located in a district zoned for higher density residential, professional offices, or commercial use, you may find that the restrictions diminish or disappear. Of course, if you buy a single-family house in a district that permits two to four units (or more), you might renovate the property into multiple units. (This possibility goes beyond this present discussion. For more on this topic, see My book *Make Money with Affordable Apartment Buildings and Commercial Properties, Second Edition* [Wiley, 2008].)

> **Should "families" receive preference in the zoning laws?**

The Family Exception Some single-family zoning districts permit accessory apartments, but only if two conditions are met: (1) The owners live in

---

[1] Remember, too, that most communities establish at least three or four distinct single-family zoning categories. Some single-family districts may permit accessory units while others do not.

the home; and (2) the person(s) who lives in the unit must be related to the property owners. Again, this type of ordinance displays an arbitrary and irrational standard. To the extent such ordinances regulate at all, they should regulate behavior, not family status. Indeed, many fair housing laws prohibit discrimination by family status, yet zoning laws, themselves, frequently discriminate along these lines.

(As an aside, federal law and the majority of state and local fair housing laws throughout the country do not apply to owner-occupied dwellings of four units or less. Consult an attorney or a local fair housing office to learn the rules in your area.)

The Mortgage Helper

As to the idea of accessory unit as mortgage helper, use this technique personally or to expand the market for a property that you're renovating to sell or rent. Here's the experience of freelance artist Andrea McKenna.

Andrea McKenna's Fixer   Andrea bought a three-story fixer and converted the lowest floor into an accessory apartment that she rented to two sisters for $350 a month. But once Andrea fully realized the income potential of her house, she carried her idea further. After the tenant sisters moved out, Andrea relocated herself to the third floor of her property. Next, she renovated both lower floors into two private units that she rented out for $550 a month each.

"I don't earn much," says Andrea, "and I doubt that I'll ever become another Andy Warhol and make a fortune. So it's great to enjoy the security of rent checks coming in. I'm now receiving $1,100 a month. That's enough to pay my mortgage and cover part of my property taxes and homeowners insurance."

> **An accessory apartment expands the market for your property.**

Buy the *Biggest* House on the Block   You've probably heard the old saw, "Never *buy* the *biggest* or most expensive house in the neighborhood." For the renovator who plans to build an accessory apartment, that advice doesn't hold. When you think income potential, the biggest house often offers the lowest price per square foot of living space.

> **The biggest house on the block can make you money.**

Say you look at an 1,800-square-foot, three-bedroom, two-bath house that's typical for the neighborhood. It's priced at $115,000. If you put 10 percent down, your mortgage payment will run $654 per month (6.5 percent, 30 years). You're interested but drive around the area and see what else you can discover. You find a 2,200-square-foot, five-bedroom, three-bath house priced at $135,000. With 10 percent down, payments for this house would cost you $768 a month. (You can easily buy properties at this price range in much of what U.S. coastal cities call "flyover country.")

Given that you see the profit potential of accessory apartments, you buy the larger house. Next, you obtain a home equity loan for $10,000 and use that money to remodel two bedrooms and a bath into an efficiency apartment. After deducting the monthly payment on your home equity loan, you clear $300 a month from the rental of the efficiency apartment. You apply that amount to your $768 mortgage payment, which brings your monthly outlay down to just $468. You enjoy three bedrooms and two baths, but they cost you much less per month. As a bonus, you build more equity with the larger house. This technique works well to enhance affordability in markets with high-priced housing, too. When you split a larger house, you might boost affordability from say, $350,000 up to as much as $500,000.

Renovate for Sale   You can use this same principle when you renovate a property for sale. Choose a larger property in a given neighborhood. Renovate with an accessory unit. The rental income increases the number of homebuyers who can afford the property. The house will cost the buyers less per month and at the same time they're able to afford a larger house and possibly a better neighborhood than they otherwise could afford. Even though your buyers receive a great deal, you still sell at a premium price.

Renovate to Lease   Say you find an 1,800-square-foot, three-bedroom, two-bath house that after renovation will rent for $1,500 a month. Rather than leave it as a single-family residence, you slice off 400 square feet to remodel as a studio apartment and a newly built bathroom. This studio rents for $650 per month. The remaining living area of 1,400 square feet with two bedrooms and two baths rents for $1,250 a month. By renting two smaller living areas instead of one larger area, you boost your total rental income by $400 per month.

> Smaller rental units typically bring higher rental revenues per square foot.

Compare rentals to determine the most profitable-sized units. But as a rule, for the same level of quality, smaller living spaces bring in more rent per square foot than do larger areas. Look for large houses or even houses with large oversized garages. Then rightsize the number, type, and square footages of the rental units to maximize rental revenue. If you buy the biggest house in the neighborhood, you often get what amounts to a quantity discount. Or you might say that you buy space wholesale and rent it out retail.

What Type of Property Works Best?

In my experience, five types of housing designs lend themselves particularly well to efficiency/studio conversions:

1.   Split level
2.   Two story with new separate exterior stair access
3.   Ranch house with split floor plan
4.   House or townhouse with a basement or lower level that opens at ground level to the backyard (usually the house front entry is at street level on a lot that slopes downhill)
5.   House with an attached garage or carport

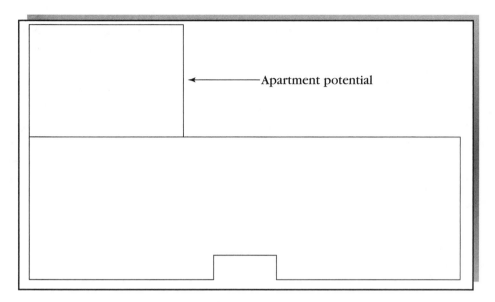

Figure 7.1 Apartment Potential.

Use your imagination, though. You can make other styles and designs work. Properties appear in an infinite range of shapes, sizes, styles, and designs. With thought and creativity, your possibilities multiply. For example, an inverted L-shaped house as shown here in Figure 7.1 can also work well.

I owned a house where a large additional unit had been built in the attic, but it lacked a fully equipped kitchen. Because building a kitchen into an attic entails considerable expense, attic conversions typically work best as areas for sleeping, studying, or playing. Depending on the configuration of the plumbing, an attic bathroom may or may not prove financially feasible.

The attic apartment in this property consisted of a bedroom, a large living area with a makeshift kitchen (counter appliances, dorm fridge), and a bathroom. Two dormers had been added to bring in more sunlight. Electric baseboard provided heat and a large window A/C unit provided air conditioning. An entry stairwell to the attic was built just inside the main front entry to the house. Originally, the previous owners of the property had built this apartment for an adult son who was living in the home. Today, with boomerang kids becoming more prevalent, apartments of this nature will experience increased popularity.

Add quality living space to a property and you increase its value. Check zoning, check comps, check costs, and run the numbers. In most cases, the extra living space will pay large profits. (For excellent illustrations of how to add extra rentable apartments to single-family houses, see Patrick Hall and Jolene Ostler, *Creating an Accessory Apartment* [McGraw-Hill, 1987].)

CHAPTER 8

Revitalize the Neighborhood

You've probably heard it said, "Buy in the best location you can afford. You can change anything about a house except its location." At first glance, this advice sounds plausible. But rethink what the term *location* actually refers to:

- ◆ Convenience (accessibility)
- ◆ Taxes/services
- ◆ Aesthetics
- ◆ Microclimate (weather)
- ◆ People: attitudes, lifestyles

- ◆ Safety and security
- ◆ Legal restrictions
- ◆ Image/reputation
- ◆ Schools
- ◆ Affordability

You can see that with the lone exception of weather, you most certainly can work to improve a property's location in dozens of specific ways.

Neighborhoods Can Get Better

The past 5 to 15 years have seen many previously "marginal" neighborhoods revitalized and gentrified—but now priced beyond the means of many first-time buyers: the Wrigley section of Long Beach, South of Market in San Francisco, South of Houston (So-Ho) in Manhattan,

Profitably improve the neighborhood.

Lincoln Park–De Paul in Chicago, and Capitol Hill in Washington, D.C., represent just a few examples. "Boy, I wish I had gotten into Rockridge (Oakland, California) ten years ago," someone recently said to me. And on my last trip to Chicago, I talked with a now-not-so-young couple who complained, "In the late eighties, we could have bought a house on a decent block in Hyde Park for less than $75,000. But we decided against it. Now you can't find anything like it for less than $250,000."

Ten to 15 years ago, every one of the abovementioned neighborhoods experienced its share of urban problems typical of larger cities. And none of these neighborhoods remains free of problems today. But each of these neighborhoods boasts revived popularity and price increases of 100 to 200 percent.

Everyone has to live somewhere.

What's more important for your future is that hundreds of somewhat similar neighborhoods are positioned for turnaround during the next 10 years. As good people are priced out of "highly desirable" neighborhoods, they move into "less desirable" neighborhoods. But that's not where the story ends. As homebuying counselor Mary Ortez tells her clients, "You have to realize you can make almost any area nicer."

Neighborhoods aren't inherently good or bad. It's the people in them and the standards and values they enforce that determine a neighborhood's future. No one encourages you to invest in a neighborhood where kids dodge gunfire as they walk to school or a neighborhood where residents post signs in their car windows, "Please don't break in. Stereo system already stolen." But standing in between the worst and best neighborhoods are many areas that are improving because local residents are working to make better lives for themselves and their families.

Wilma Haynes, former chairman of the Watts Property Owners Association, says, "People who come to Watts are very surprised at what they see. All around me people have fixed up their houses, bought lots that have sat vacant for years, and are feeling pride in their neighborhood."

Will Williams, co-developer of a subdivision in Watts, says,

We have brought back to Watts those people who moved out to rent in Gardenia and Inglewood, people who became tired of driving back in from Palmdale and Rialto, people who moved back to the neighborhood where their mama still lives. We've built nice enough homes to give them a reason to come back to Watts. There's no reason you can't put up nice homes here. Watts deserves decent homes as much as any other place.

> **High prices have pushed buyers and investors to search for properties in lower-priced locations.**

The problems and revitalization of Watts have been well publicized; the advantages have not. "It's the only affordable area close in," says one buyer. Others point out that the neighborhood sits right next to the University of Southern California. And, several years back, when property prices stalled in much of Los Angeles, prices in Watts continued to go up and its sales outpaced other parts of the city.

In an article on homebuying, *Money Magazine* advised its readers, "It's a great time to shop for your dream house. . . . Seek out the neighborhoods where property values are rising faster than your community average." Surprising to many investors, though, is the fact that the neighborhoods where prices are positioned to rise fastest may not be the most prestigious or well-established neighborhoods. Often, areas poised for turnaround or renewed popularity present the best opportunity for quick gain. When you combine market appreciation with renovation, such neighborhoods give fixers and flippers a double dose of profit potential.

Entrepreneurs Improve Thorton Park (and Make a Killing)

"Florida's new urban entrepreneurs can envision a bustling district of sushi bars, loft apartments, and boutiques where now sits a glass-strewn lot or rat-infested warehouse," says Cynthia Barret.

> **Discover neighborhoods that will gentrify within the next decade.**

Phil Rampy is proud to have been one of those early entrepreneurs. Since Rampy bought his house in the then-shunned Thorton Park neighborhood near trash-strewn Lake Eola (or as they used to call it, Lake Erie-ola), Thorton Park has climbed up the status ladder to rank among "the trendiest addresses" in Orlando. That $60,000 bungalow that Rampy renovated is now valued at close to $250,000. Although the Thorton Park neighborhood still sits on this Earth in the same place as it always has, nearly everything else about this location has changed.

Every Neighborhood Has Potential

When you compare neighborhoods, look beyond the present. Imagine potential. List a neighborhood's good points. How could you and other property owners join together to highlight and improve these features? List the neighborhood's weak points. How can you and others eliminate negative influences? Whom can you enlist to promote your cause? Can you mobilize mortgage lenders, other investors, homeowners, realtors, not-for-profit housing groups, church leaders, builders, contractors, preservationists, police, local employers, retail businesses, schoolteachers, principals, community redevelopment agencies, elected officials, civic groups, and perhaps students, professors, and administrators of a nearby college or university?

Throughout the United States, people like you have joined with other property owners and tenants to revitalize and reinvigorate hundreds of neighborhoods. From South of Market in San Francisco, to the Madison Valley in Seattle, Lakeview in Chicago, Boston's North End, Manhattan's Bowery and So-Ho, Miami's South Beach, and the "M Street" neighborhoods in Dallas, in all of these locations neighbors, merchants, investors, and homebuyers have organized campaigns to make living, working, and shopping in these areas much more desirable. "We liked the community," says homebuyer Roy Owens

> **Learn what people say about different neighborhoods.**

of Cumberland (Atlanta), "but we felt the community association was too passive. It needed some *oomph,* so we incorporated and worked hard to get to know people and inspire them to get involved."

In speaking of a San Diego neighborhood that's headed for turna-round and redevelopment, Lori Weisberg says, "To the outsider, there's little here that seems inviting. . . . Yet, where most people see a shabby area . . . forward-looking investors envision an exciting new downtown neighborhood adorned with a grand, tree-lined boulevard, a central plaza, artisans' studios, loft housing, and crowned with a sports and entertainment center. . . . [Already] you can see pockets of gentrifica-tion—a budding arts district, scattered loft conversions, and . . . struc-tures well-suited for preservation. . . . But [the complete revitalization and redevelopment] does have to be imagined."

"There's no doubt," says an executive with San Diego's Centre City Development Corporation, "This project is happening—it's just a ques-tion of when it will all come together."

How can this executive express such certainty that this revitali-zation will occur? Because when people join together to bring about positive change, neighborhoods improve. Everybody wins with a better quality of life and increased property values.

Community Action and Community Spirit Make a Difference

In his review of the book, *Safe Homes, Safe Neighborhoods* (NOLO, 1993), real estate investor, attorney, columnist, and book reviewer Robert Bruss, says, "This is an action book. . . . This is a welcome and long-overdue book for activists who want to learn how to improve their neighborhood." This book illustrates perfectly how through community action and community spirit people can improve the quality of their neighbor-hoods and their lives. Without a doubt, many city and suburban neighborhoods must tackle prob-lems of one sort or another. Besides crime, these problems may range from barking dogs to speed-ing high schoolers to a lack of parks, sidewalks, or

> **Community action can conquer crime and criminals.**

storm sewers. Yet, regardless of the specific problems to be solved (or prevented), as urban entrepreneur Tony Goldman proved with Miami's South Beach, people acting together can make a difference.

"While it may seem that everywhere crime is on the rise," write Stephanie Mann and M.C. Blakeman *(Safe Homes, Safe Neighborhoods),* "in many neighborhoods the opposite is true. In cities and towns across the country, local crime prevention groups have reduced burglaries and car break-ins; helped catch muggers, rapists, and kidnappers; established Block Parents and other child-safety projects; driven out drug dealers; eliminated graffiti; and, in general, made their homes and streets safer. All it takes is a few people to get things started. By identifying and focusing on a neighborhood's main concerns—and working with police and each other—neighbors can make a difference."

> **Fix broken windows.**

Become a Neighborhood *Entrepreneur*

You don't have to live in a big-trouble, inner-city location to become an urban entrepreneur. You can do it anywhere. No neighborhood is perfect. I suspect that even Beverly Hills and Scarsdale could stand improvement in at least a few ways.

> **Values jump with neighborhood improvements.**

Since neighborhood quality drives up property values and rent levels, initiate (or join in) to make a neighborhood a better place to live. When you simultaneously improve your property(ies) *and* its location, you more than double your profit potential. Act on these suggestions and you add value to your properties.

Boost Neighborhood Convenience and Accessibility

Would a stoplight, wider road, or new highway interchange improve accessibility to the neighborhood? Where are the to-and-fro traffic logjams? How can they be alleviated? Is the neighborhood served as well as it could be by buses and commuter trains? How about social service transportation? Could you get the vans that pick up seniors or the disabled to place this neighborhood on their route? What about the traveling bus for the library? Does it stop in the neighborhood?

Maybe resident efforts could pull more employers, health-care services, restaurants, or coffee houses into the neighborhood. Could you convert that old warehouse or industrial building into loft apartments, live/work studios, or professional offices? Remember, you can add convenience to a neighborhood in two ways: (1) Make travel to and from the neighborhood easier, cheaper, or more timely; or (2) bring more shops, services, nightlife, culture, jobs, and recreational facilities into the neighborhood.

> **Try to attract new retailers, coffee houses, and restaurants.**

Improve Appearances and Aesthetics

Put together a civic pride organization. Organize a cleanup and fix-up campaign. Plant trees, shrubs, and flowers in yards and in public areas. Lobby the city to tear down or eliminate eyesore buildings, graffiti, or trashy areas. Reduce on-street parking. Get undrivable or abandoned vehicles towed. Enforce environmental regulations against property owners and businesses that pollute (noise, smoke, odors). Walk the neighborhood. What eyesores do you notice? Do what's necessary to alleviate them.

> **Fix-up becomes contagious.**

In fact, as you fix up your yard and buildings, you motivate other owners to enhance their own properties. Here's what nationally syndicated columnist and longtime real estate investor Robert Bruss reports:

> Fixing up houses spurs a contagious effect. You will be amazed at how, within a few months after you fix up your house, the neighborhood owners will begin fixing up their

properties. To illustrate, recently I completed fixing up a foreclosure property I acquired a few months ago. Before I was
even finished, the next door neighbor (who has lived there
over 20 years!) began painting and landscaping his house.
"You shamed me into doing it," Manuel told me. He also owns
a rental house across the street which he cleaned and painted. Another neighbor tells me he plans to paint his rundown
house because now he noticed how bad it looks. All it takes is
one or two owners fixing up their houses and the neighbors
catch the fix-up fever! As a result, the whole neighborhood
increases in market value.[1]

Amen!

Zoning and Building Regulations

Are property owners in the neighborhood splitting up single-family
houses and converting them into apartments? Do residents run businesses out of their homes and garages? Are high- or midrise buildings
planned that will diminish livability? Are commercial properties en-
croaching on the area? Then lobby for tighter zon-
ing and building regulations. Or from the opposite
perspective, does the neighborhood seem ripe for
more intense development? Then lobby the city to
rezone the area to apartments or commercial.

> **Enlist the help
> of the code
> enforcers.**

(In Gainesville, FL, near the UF campus, the
city has rezoned older, rundown SFR neighbor-
hoods to multifamily. Investors are flocking in to buy houses, tear them
down, and build low- to mid-rise $300,000 condominiums and upscale
apartment projects.)

Because zoning and building regulations control property use,
they alter property values. When value-creating changes are warranted,
pressure the politicians and planners to accommodate this need.

---

[1] Quoted from the Robert Bruss Real Estate Newsletter, #92215 (p. 2).

Eliminate Neighborhood Nuisances

Do some households in the neighborhood make a nuisance of themselves? Junk cars in the driveway, barking dogs, loud stereos, vehicles without noise-reducing mufflers, constant yelling and shouting, out-of-control yards littered with debris—you and other property owners can force them to clean up their act or suffer severe and continuing penalties.

Invoke Your Local Ordinances, Deed Restrictions, or HOA Rules

Pore over local ordinances, deed restrictions, and homeowners' association (HOA) rules. Sift through the regulations for zoning, aesthetics, occupancy, use, parking, noise, disturbing the peace, health, safety, loitering, drug-dealing or possession, extortion, and assault. You can surely find some ordinance or rule violations under which you (and others) can make yourselves heard.

> **Rules seldom permit nuisances to continue if residents jointly complain.**

If after receiving a citation the people continue to offend common decency, a judge can issue an order to cease and desist (or something similar). Further violations would then bring a citation for contempt of court. They've now angered the judge. Each day the breach persists could rack up multiple fines and possibly jail time. In some cases, the government will remedy the problem—cut the weeds, haul off a junk car—and bill the offenders. If they don't pay, it becomes a lien against the property. If the offenders are tenants, file a complaint against the landlord (owner). Increasingly, cities can fine landlords when they fail to place law-abiding tenants in their properties.

Sue in Small Claims Court

Although you can petition a judge to force inconsiderate neighbors to comply with local ordinances, you need not rely on this approach. Except in Louisiana, the common law provides another recourse. It's called

> **Judges can force people to comply with the law.**

the *tort* (legal wrong) *of nuisance.* With or without a specific ordinance, you can sue your offensive neighbor(s) in small claims court (no lawyer, low filing fees) for committing a nuisance.

The esteemed jurist Blackstone defined a nuisance as "Any thing that unlawfully worketh hurt, inconvenience, or damage." In modern times, an Illinois court has said that nuisance includes "everything that endangers life or health, gives offense to the senses, violates the laws of decency, or obstructs reasonable and comfortable use of a property."

Reasonable   To sue for nuisance, show that: (1) The neighbor's conduct *unreasonably* offends you or your tenants and/or harms the value of your property; and (2) your complaint does not run afoul of common sense or community standards. In other words, if a neighboring property owner's children play loudly, scream, and carry on as kids do, you won't stand much chance of winning your case. Nevertheless, whenever you can persuade a jury of your peers that you're not merely oversensitive, you will likely prevail. (Unless the defendant can claim some constitutional or statutory protection. For example, absent some type of aesthetics ordinance or HOA rule, the rights of property typically permit people to paint—or not paint—their house any way they choose.)

Dollar Damages   Although most *small claims court* judges can't issue "clean up your act" orders, they will award damages to the person who wins his or her case. If the offender (defendant) still fails to follow the straight and narrow, you can go back into court and sue repeatedly for as many times as necessary. Each case you win means more damages that the offender must pay.

> **People who refuse to "cease and desist" can suffer multiple fines or claims for damages.**

In your small claims suit, you can name a property owner whose tenants are creating the problem. Some short-sighted landlords care only about collecting rent—not protecting the interests of the neighborhood. A court judgment will sober them up. If the wayward landlords don't pay the court-ordered damages, you can place a lien against their property.

Your suit does not preclude other neighborhood property owners or tenants who suffer harm from also suing those inconsiderate tortfeasors. A sequence of nuisance suits will likely bring scalawag landlords and tenants into line.[2]

Upgrade the Schools

The *Wall Street Journal* (August 23, 2001) reports that "parents and property owners have become increasingly aggressive about trying to improve their public schools." When you think that in many areas parents spend $3,000 to $10,000 a year to send their kids to private schools, why not rechannel those monies and support into the neighborhood schools?

> **Improve school performance and watch property values set new highs.**

In some cases, a neighborhood school may not deserve its dismal reputation. Or perhaps a strong-performing school (at least in some area of specialization) isn't receiving the favorable notice it deserves. So, spread the word through publicity and press releases. Let potential homebuyers, tenants, and realty agents know the good news. Because better schools and school reputations boost property values, neighborhood improvement can easily begin with upgrading the schools.

Safety and Security

You can reduce neighborhood crime (see *Safe Home, Safe Neighborhoods*), and you can eliminate dangerous traffic flows within the

---

[2]For a comprehensive discussion of neighbor law, see Mark Warda, *Neighbor vs. Neighbor* (Sphinx Publishing, 1991); also, *Neighbor Law* (Nolo Press, Berkeley, CA, 2005).

neighborhood (especially for children and seniors). Slow down or reroute traffic. If you can get the city to lay down speed bumps, you achieve both objectives at the same time. Speed bumps not only force motorists to let up on the gas pedal, they tell drivers who want to speed that they better travel a different street.

Also, post lower speed limits and petition for strict enforcement. In Berkeley, California, several neighborhoods lobbied the city to erect traffic barriers at residential intersections. This effort blocked formerly drive-through streets.

Petition the Politicians

Property owners pay taxes. Insist that you receive what you pay for. As the Berkeley experience proves, when property owners and neighborhood residents join together to form a political force, they can push the city politicos to alleviate traffic problems, clean the streets, enforce ordinances, upgrade the schools, beef up police patrols, create parks, and provide other services that neighborhoods should expect.

> **Insist on the government services for which you and other property owners pay taxes.**

Of course, the politicos alone can't achieve neighborhood goals. They need the continued assistance of community groups. City measures work most effectively when combined with self-help. If no neighborhood action groups now exist, spearhead their formation or revival.

Add Luster to Your Image

Some friends of mine used to live in Miami, Florida, but now they live in the upscale Village of Pinecrest, Florida. Did they move? No; they and their neighbors persuaded the post office to give them a new address so

> **Give your neighborhood or community a new name.**

they could distinguish themselves from that diverse agglomeration known as Miami. As part of their efforts to create an improved neighborhood, some residents of Sepulveda have formed a new community and renamed it North Hill. In Maryland, Gaithersburg has changed its name to North Potomac, attempting to capitalize on the prestige of its nearby neighbor. Some residents of North Hollywood got the official name of part of their community changed to Valley Village. "With the name change," says realtor Jerry Burns, "residents take more pride in their neighborhood."

Accent Something Special

As another idea to shine up the image of a neighborhood, accent or create something special. This "something special" could stand out as the sincere friendliness of St. Johns or Brentwood; the art deco architecture of South Beach; the rural feeling—"It's like an oasis in the big city. We have owls living in our trees and all kinds of animals"—of places like

> **Publicize neighborhood strengths.**

Montecito Heights or Rogers Point; the waterfront of Marina Bay; the ethnic diversity of Richmond Annex; the American heritage of the historical district in Annapolis; or the Victorians of Hyde Park.

Create and accent a "something special" theme for the neighborhood. You boost property values.

Talk Up the Neighborhood

Most people learn about various neighborhoods through word of mouth and articles they read in newspapers and magazines. As all good publicists know, you can influence "getting the word out." Talk up the area to opinion leaders. Comment to friends, co-workers, relatives, and acquaintances about the relative housing bargains and the great improvements (or underappreciated assets) of the community.

Persuade a reporter to write about or broadcast the neighborhood's potential for turnaround, quality of life, convenience, or affordability. Let everyone know that the area deserves attention as a good area to buy a home or invest in property.

Get the Banks Involved (Affordability)

To meet their obligations under the Community Reinvestment Act (CRA), some mortgage lenders work to revitalize urban areas. One could say that instead of "redlining," lenders are now "greenlining." They target communities and neighborhoods for easier-qualifying mortgages and property improvement loans. Instead of pulling out of these areas, some mortgage lenders pour money into them.

> **The CRA requires banks to invest in neighborhoods where they accept branch deposits.**

> **Locate neighborhoods that are attracting an increasing percentage of homebuyers.**

For example, under a homeownership initiative struck by the city of Dallas, a group of participating mortgage lenders, and Fannie Mae, 15,000 renters who buy a house within the city limits of Dallas—and in some instances, within targeted neighborhoods—became eligible for special financing programs, which include grants and loans for down payments, closing costs, lease-purchase programs, flexible underwriting standards, property improvement loans, and homebuyer counseling (to be offered in both English and Spanish).

When mortgage financing becomes available, many neighborhoods become positioned for turnaround. With more money available, residents who rent today will buy tomorrow. Then, as these homeowners renovate and remodel their properties, the character of the neighborhood improves. To identify turnaround potential, discover those neighborhoods where community redevelopment or community reinvestment monies are scheduled to flow. As investors, homeowners, tenants, and community groups revitalize their neighborhoods, the equity in your property will multiply in value.

Buy on the Bad News

A stock market axiom advises, "Buy on the bad news, sell on the good news." (Or stated more colorfully, "Buy with the sound of the canons, sell with the triumph of the trumpets.") When bad news or a pessimistic mood prevails, bargains are ripe for the pickings. With bad news all around, sellers outnumber buyers.

This same advice holds for neighborhood "stigma" or other types of bad news. If a neighborhood is poised for turnaround but hasn't yet lost its reputation, you can look forward to strong price gains as improvements take hold and the good word begins to spread.

Baron de Rothschild urged investors to buy when they see "blood running in the streets." As to investing in neighborhoods, I wouldn't follow that advice literally. But, no doubt, the past decade's escalation of housing prices has shut many first-time homebuyers out of many neighborhoods and communities that seemed affordable prior to the late 1990s.

Each year for the next 15 years, four million echo boomers will pour into the housing market. Fixing up neighborhoods will become a national pastime. Property investors, homeowners, citizen groups, not-for-profits, businesses, and city government now recognize that community improvement pays big dividends for everyone. To gain these sure profits, fix up your own properties. But go further. Work to improve, renovate, and revitalize neighborhoods.

> **The echo boomers will flock to affordable neighborhoods.**

CHAPTER 9

Market Your Property for Top Dollar

Now pocket your reward. You renovate your property to wow potential buyers or tenants. You revitalize the neighborhood. You know that the property will virtually sell itself. Your value proposition offers a better deal than competing properties. All you need to do is:

1. Go to Home Depot and buy a small $1.98 cardboard FOR SALE (or FOR RENT) sign.
2. Write your telephone number on the sign with a no. 3 pencil or light blue ball point pen.
3. Stick the sign in the front yard of the property.
4. Run a two-line classified ad in your city's major newspaper.

Presto! A line of prospects will show up. Each one will carry a checkbook in one hand and a mortgage preapproval letter in the other. You merely select the lucky buyer (tenant)—or maybe you put the property up for bid. The prospects fight each other for the privilege of owning (or leasing) this property. You end up with a sales price $50,000 higher than you were asking (or much higher rents).

> **Properties rarely sell themselves for top dollar.**

If you think such an easy and rewarding sale (or rental) sounds like fantasy, you're right. Yet many sellers and landlords do believe they can sell (rent) their property with similarly inadequate marketing techniques. Even when you renovate a property to dazzle your prospects, you can't put promotion on autopilot. To earn the highest profits, plan your sales efforts just as you planned the property improvements.

Later in this chapter, you'll see the pros and cons of using a real estate agent to sell (or rent) your properties. For now, assume that you offer the property by owner. Even when you employ a real estate agent (or property management company), these marketing pointers will help you guide and evaluate the work of your agent.

Whom Do You Want to Reach?

As you designed your renovations, you chose a target market of buyers or tenants. Who are these people? Where do they work? Where do they shop? What publications do they read? What clubs, organizations, and trade or professional associations do they belong to? What churches do they attend? In what colleges are they enrolled? Do they have friends, co-workers, or relatives who live in the neighborhood? What social service agencies cater to their needs? What do their demographics and psychographics look like?

> **Publicize your property where you can most effectively reach your target market.**

Why So Many Questions?

You answer these and similar questions because you do not want to waste time, money, and effort shotgunning promotions and sales messages. You want to rent or sell this property with the least amount of time, effort, and expense. To avoid working harder and wasting advertising dollars, work smarter. The more you know about your potential prospects, the better you can figure out where to spread the word about your property and what to say. Why spend to advertise in a newspaper if a well-written notice on a bulletin board immediately makes your telephone ring?

Sell Benefits, Not Just the Property

As you think about whom to reach, remember the maxim, "People don't buy features, they buy benefits." Yet many property owners fail to plan their message. They take five minutes to jot down the basic features of their property. Then they phone in an ad to a newspaper. What results is nothing more than a generic, unexciting property description such as the following:

> **Sell the sizzle *and* the steak.**

Park Terrace: Split plan, 3-br, 2-bth, den, 2-car garage, 1,650 sq. ft., large lot, close to schools and shopping. For more information, call (555)123-4567 after 5:00 P.M. No realtors!

Standing by itself, this ad may seem okay. But standing in the classified section of a newspaper surrounded by hundreds of other ads, it does nothing to grab the target buyer's attention and shout, "Here's the home you've been looking for. Here's why you will want to phone about this property right now."

To draw targeted buyers into the ad and motivate them to call, emphasize benefits. Don't trust the buyer's imagination. Don't think that if prospects want more information they will call. There's too much advertising competition. Prospects seldom call just to get more information. They call only when out of all the ads they looked through, your ad excited them enough to make the final cut.

Advertising pros tell sellers to organize and write their ads to "sell the sizzle, not just the steak." Describe a property's features in a way that presses your prospect's hot buttons. Sergeant Friday may be pleased with "Just the facts, Ma'am." But you need to sell the sizzle.

Sell the Sizzle

So, that returns us to the questions:

1. Who are your prospects?
2. What benefits do you offer that distinguish your property from competing properties?

Are your prospects looking for one or more of these benefits?

- Bright with natural light
- Spacious open floor plan, wonderful for entertaining
- Quiet street
- Home warranty, no repair costs for at least two years
- Top-rated school district
- Unlimited storage space
- Bargain price
- Mortgage helper in-suite
- Warranted new roof
- Great appreciation potential
- Low cost of upkeep
- Choose your own cabinets, carpets, and colors
- Drop-dead gorgeous kitchen and bathrooms
- Totally private setting
- Owner will carry financing
- Safe and secure neighborhood
- Prestigious address/community
- Energy-saving, low utility bills
- Lowest price in neighborhood
- Low down payment
- Seller pays closing costs
- Walk to shops, cafes, and restaurants
- Easy-qualifying assumable financing
- Serene views
- Immaculate condition, pride of ownership

Go through your property and list every feature and benefit that will excite your buyers (tenants). Which of these features and benefits will motivate your prospects to call? Which of these desirable features and benefits are rarely found in competitive properties? When you strategically craft your improvements, you can strategically craft a sales message that gets your property sold (or rented).

Crafting a Newspaper Ad

To save money, many sellers cut their classified ads too short. They list a few cold property facts and then expect prospects to call for more information. Don't waste time and money with such meager efforts. If you advertise in a newspaper, include the following information:

- ◆ Sizzling hot buttons
- ◆ Square footage
- ◆ Room count
- ◆ Street address
- ◆ Price

- ◆ Terms, if any
- ◆ Amenities
- ◆ Open house hours
- ◆ Lot size/landscaping
- ◆ Telephone number/web site

As an owner-seller, you cannot use the same tactics that many real estate agencies follow. Contrary to what people believe, real estate firms do not run house-for-sale ads to sell specific houses. They run ads to generate prospects for agents. Once an agent hooks the prospect, they set off to tour a number of properties. Eventually, the agent hopes to sell some property, but they don't particularly care which one (except they do prefer to sell their own listings).

> **The better you tell, the more you sell.**

You're marketing just one property; you can't effectively shotgun your sales message. If you do not hit your targeted buyers with the benefits they're looking for, they won't circle your ad. Or with a misdirected or sparsely worded ad, you may get calls from tire kickers, looky-loos, and people who want something other than what you're selling. Poor advertising (especially when linked with overpricing) explains why most for-sale-by-owners fail to sell their properties and end up listing with a Realtor. Compare and contrast the actual ads shown in Figure 9.1.

The ads in the right-hand column of the figure entice their prospective buyers far better than the ads on the left. Ad #1 does try to score with hot button owner financing but omits essential pricing and qualifying information in favor of "call to qualify." Ad #2 also accents the "owner finance" benefit but omits the amount of the down payment, monthly payments, qualifying standards, and enticing information

1. **LAKE FOREST Lease Option/ Owner Financing.** Gated community 4BR/3.5BR, fplc. Luxury pool. Home built in 2000. 2600 sf home on child-safe cul-de-sac. Move-in now! Call to pre-qualify. 1-987-654-3210.

2. **ORLANDO**—4br/2.5ba 2572sf, 2 car garage, owner will finance. $219,950. Call 1-987-654-3210.

3. **OCOEE HILLS**—3/1.5. CHA. Large corner lot, must sell. $84,500. Please call 1-987-654-3210.

4. **DELAND**—4 br ba brick hm, firepl, 2 car gar. Scrn pool & patio. Excel area. Call 1-987-654-3210.

5. **CLERMONT/GREATER PINES**—3/2 w/den. New schools. Call owner for more info. 1-987-654-3210.

6. **ALTAMONTE SPRINGS/LAKE ORIENTA**—FSBO, 3/2, 5, 2, 2300sf, scrn pool/Jacuzzi, $299,995. 1-987-654-3210.

7. **LONGWOOD/MARKHAM WOODS**—Private 5/3.5, 3620sf + 600sf office/apt., 1.6 acre, pool/spa, 2700sf scrnd lanai, gourmet kit, huge master, best schls. $425K. 1-987-654-3210.

8. **DR. PHILLIPS/TURTLE CREEK**— Gated. Corner Lot, 3/2.5 w/Loft, gorgeous landscaped 1 acre. Master Down, Pool, Model Condition, Fabulous Kitchen w/Island, Courtyard. Lowest Price in Turtle Creek, $288,900. 1-987-654-3210.

9. **THE VILLAGES**—2/2, corner lot, 1990 site built, sun porch, W/D, new carpet, paint, across from pool. Survey, termite/house inspections & treatments include. $99,500. Open House, 808 St. Andrews Blvd. 1-987-654-3210.

10. **CLERMONT**—Lake view, Fl living at its affordable best. Saw Mill Subdiv, 1,836 sf, 3br/2ba, walk-in closets, Jacuzzi tub/mstr bath, blt 1997. 3/4 corner lot. Beautiful established lawn, priv. fence, spacious liv rm w/vaulted ceiling, dining rm, fam/great rm. You'll love the kitchen, breakfast rm, ofc area. 2 car gar, attic storage. New school to be constructed nearby. Gated, security patrolled. $174,900. 1-987-654-3210.

Figure 9.1 Advertisements.

to sell the sizzle of the property itself. Ads #3 through #6 illustrate the Joe Friday "just the facts" minimalist approach. Little in any of these sales messages attempts to excite or motivate targeted buyers. In fact, ad #5 wastes a full line by stating the obvious, "Call owner for more info."

Rather than telling people to call for more info, spark their enthusiasm to call with feature/benefit enticements. The ad on the following page illustrates how to draft an effective sales message.

Notice how this ad blends facts and benefits. It conveys comparative advantage (a value proposition that beats competitors) and it implies the need to "jump on this one" before it's gone.

Affordable—Spacious—Stunning

Mint condition. 3/2, 1,840 sq. ft. $6,000 d.p., $830 per mo., romantic 400 sq. ft. Mstr. BR suite with fplc., open living area, flower garden views, light and bright kitchen delight, unlimited storage. $360,000—compare at $385,000! 210 Pecan. Open Sat. & Sun. 12-5. 987-555-1234.

This ad composition follows the well-known format of *AIDA*:

◆ Attention (headlined benefits)
◆ Interest (condition and affordability)
◆ Desire (prized features and benefits)
◆ Action (open house, rare bargain, please call)

This ad will make the phone ring with motivated buyers. If you deliver as promised, you'll sell the first weekend.

A Word about Price   This ad prices the property at $360,000, yet it invites the prospect to compare with homes priced at $385,000. Does this mean that you're giving the property away? No.

Advertise a good price.

Except in super-hot markets, sellers who have listed their property with a real estate firm at $385,000 will likely accept an offer of, say, $362,500 to $367,500. Subtract a sales commission and the seller nets somewhere around $355,000. So you net about the same amount (or more) while making a quicker sale and still give your buyer a good deal on the stunning home that you created from a lump of coal.

Update your comp price data.

Recheck the Market   You toured comp homes and scoured the for-sale ads before you bought and renovated your property. But that was probably three to six months ago. Now, before you write your ad and settle on an asking price, recheck the market. Go through some of the open houses in competitive neighborhoods.

Read the ads for these properties. Note strengths and weaknesses vis-à-vis your property. Then craft your ad and your asking price to accent your property's advantages. Houses sell within a competitive market. Always know what your competitors offer, what prices they ask, and the sizzle of their sales message.

Prepare a Property Brochure or Flyer

Although well-crafted newspaper ads can sometimes prove effective, also prepare an advertising brochure or flyer like those you see hanging in tubes beneath for-sale signs. Again, though, give your sales message some sizzle. Avoid the bland random lists of features as shown in Figures 9.1, 9.2, and 9.3. These actual flyers illustrate how *not* to write a sales message.

Lazy Agent's Flyer   Figure 9.1 shows the lazy agent's way to prepare a flyer. Simply photocopy the Multiple Listing Service (MLS) property description form. This flyer recites sterile facts and then gratuitously throws in a few benefits without elaboration. I looked at this house. It was immaculate inside and provided drop-dead gorgeous views from the living area and the master bedroom (full glass exterior wall) to a beautifully landscaped backyard. Yet the agent does not mention this unique and desirable selling point.

> **Brochures and flyers provide a highly effective, low-cost way to motivate your prospects.**

The flyer also fails to include information about the neighborhood. We learn that the roof is shingle, but nothing about its age or condition. The buyers will receive a warranty, but what will it cover, for how long, and for what amounts? As for selling points that distinguish this house from competitors, again nothing. Not even a photo. Interior and exterior photos should always play a starring role in your flyers for two reasons: (1) to show the property in a favorable pose, and (2) to provide a memory jog to prospects.

Potential buyers often grab a flyer from the for-sale sign tube but then do not look at it again for several days. By then they may have also collected a half-dozen or more other flyers. Unless the prospects already know the property and the neighborhood, their recollections will fade. And with no strong selling message, the buyers will likely place this property at the bottom of their priorities.

The Agent-Designed Flyer   Figure 9.2 shows an agent-designed flyer. Rather than photocopy the MLS form, at least this agent took 10 minutes to design and write his own flyer. What's interesting here is that the owner is also the agent. You would think that an owner-agent could do a better job than this boring property flyer. Except for the last paragraph, the listing of the property's basic description and features could just as well have been taken from the MLS form.

Omits Important Features   As to the most important home features such as style (*DET* stands for detached single-family house, which is not really an architectural style), floor plan, kitchen quality and design, ceiling height, natural light, and quality of bathrooms, this promo piece falls short. Indeed, look at the bland list under Interior and Exterior—facts, boring and mainly trivial facts. Not one feature translated into a benefit or a selling message and theme.

Confuses with Classified Adspeak   Now look at that last paragraph. What's the first thing you notice about this feeble attempt to create an enticing description of the property? It's written in run-together all caps—classified adspeak. It's close to unreadable.

When you write a flyer, you're not paying by the word or the line. Forget the choppy, abbreviated classified adspeak. Spell out your words and write in short descriptive phrases that relate to specific benefits. And definitely never write using all capital letters. Not only do capitals make reading more difficult, they look amateurish.

Deceptive Description   As a final point that the flyer only hints at ($2,500 carpet/wallpaper allowance), the house, itself, contradicts its description as "beautiful." In fact, the interior was a wreck with a garbled

3814 NW 21ST AVENUE, CAPITOL CITY, FL

Photo

$184,900

Style of Home: DET   **Apx Year Built:** 1967
Bedrooms: 4   **Full Baths:** 2
Half Baths: 1   **Square Ft:** 2221

Features

Interior	Exterior
Window Coverings	Open Patio
Crown Molding	Screened Porch/Room
Fireplace	Swim Pool-In Ground
Ceiling Fan	Sprinkler System

Remarks: BEAUTIFUL BRICK HOME IN KINGSMILL FOR THE ACTIVE FAMILY. NICE YARD WITH POOL. CONVERTED GARAGE HOUSES REC RM, OFFICE W/2 PHONE LINES & STORAGE RM. $2500 CARPET/WALLPAPER ALLOWANCE. AHS SELECT HOME WARRANTY. 2 MILES TO COLLEGE. JJ FINLEY, WESTWOOD, GHS. OWNER/AGENT.

Listed By:
JOHNSON REALTY CORP
ALVA BEMER
(456) 789-1234

Info Deemed Reliable but not Guaranteed

Figure 9.2   Agent-Designed Flyer.

floor plan and 20-year-old appliances. The postage-stamp swimming pool lacked a screen cover and seemed much more a liability than an amenity. As to that "converted garage rec room," I wish you could have seen it.

Do you recall our discussion about the quality of conversions dramatically affecting their value? To "convert" this garage, the owner had done nothing more than lay down indoor/outdoor carpet, tack up thin, cheap wall paneling, and install a suspended ceiling. Even worse, the owner/agent included this space in the 2,221-square-foot figure shown on the flyer and on the property listing sheet. When I looked at this property, it had already been on the market for more than four months. At that time, most houses in that neighborhood were selling in less than 30 days.

> **Your flyer won't sell if the property doesn't deliver.**

Overpriced Lemon   Let's go back to price per square foot as a guide to value. Most comp houses in this area were selling at around $80 per square foot. Using this measure and the 2,221-square-foot figure, you can come up with a value of $177,680 for this property. Since most comp houses didn't have pools and the owner here was willing to pay a $2,500 decorating allowance, the asking price might *appear* reasonable to some buyers.

Never fall for such a rationale. Price per square foot (psf) gives you a guide. It does not reveal the true quality of the living space. That's your job. And that's why you need to inspect comp houses before you apply their per-square-foots to properties that you value. The quality of space in this property was so poor (condition and design) that no one should have paid more than $60 to $65 psf or a purchase price somewhere around $140,000. At $180,000 the property stands as an overpriced lemon.

By-Owner Flyer   After reviewing the two agent-prepared flyers, you can easily see that the by-owner sales sheet in Figure 9.3 also fails to provide persuasive copy:

1. *Never give "For Sale by Owner" such a dominating position.* Use an attention-grabbing headline that conveys a strong benefit to the targeted buyers.
2. *Place one or more photos of the property on the flyer.* Photos jog the prospect's memory, and if done well, can accent the sales message. Use a digital camera and print color flyers from your computer. Black-and-white photocopies cheapen the property.
3. *Organize your information in related sections.* Emphasize the strongest features and benefits.
4. *Explain possibilities.* Notice that this property is zoned commercial. What does that mean for the value and uses of the property? Do not leave property potential to the buyer's imagination. (Of course, as an entrepreneurial renovator, actively search for properties that offer potential that sellers either do not recognize or undervalue.)

> **Your sales message must cut through the clutter.**

To consistently earn your highest returns, extol the advantages of your property. Otherwise, those people who would value your property most highly will zip right past your ad. How many sales messages hit you and everyone else every day? At least hundreds, maybe thousands. To persuasively motivate your prospects, your sales message must cut through the advertising glut that engulfs us.

> **Emphasize the facts and benefits that will most appeal to your market.**

Rewrite of the By-Owner Flyer Now read through my rewrite (Figure 9.4) of the by-owner flyer (Figure 9.3). First notice that I raised the price. Why? Because the owner thought that he was trying to sell a run-down property. In contrast, I'm selling the promise of making money. When the present lacks obvious appeal, sell the future.

Also notice that I've packed this flyer with facts and benefits. Experience proves that the more you tell, the more you sell. Look at any successful

FOR SALE or RENT

BY OWNER

4000 NW 6th Street

---

4 Bedroom / 2 Bath

approx. **1550 sq. ft.**

Large corner lot with 6 ft. wood privacy fence in
  backyard

Central Heat and A/C (one bedroom has separate wall
  mount A/C)

Appliances: Washer, Dryer, Refrigerator, Stove

Ceiling fans in each room

Zoned: Office/Residential (currently residential)

FOR SALE
$85,000

FOR RENT
$975 / month

Available 11-15
(First, Last and $500 Security deposit required)

Figure 9.3 By-Owner Flyer.

Cosmetic Fixer ◆ Bargain Price
◆ Loaded with Profit Potential

4000 NW 6th St. — 4/2/1550 sq. ft.
$95,000 — Terms Possible

Photo	Photo	Photo

Zoned Office/Residential – Great Income Property
with Rehab/Conversion Upside

Location	*Exterior and Site*	*Interior*
◆ Growing high-traffic corridor	◆ Low maintenance concrete block	◆ Easy office conversion
◆ 5 minutes or less to downtown, the university, major retail	◆ 4-year-old roof	◆ In-suite possibility
◆ 3% office vacancy rate in area	◆ 1/2 acre lot with up to 12-car parking	◆ Plaster soundproof walls
◆ Neighborhood revitalization in progress	◆ Building expansion possible	◆ Nearly new energy-efficient heat/AC

My Loss, Your Gain:

Owner relocation.
Lowest price per sq. ft. in area.
Will sell, lease, or lease option.

Make offer.

Cosmetic fix-up will net you a high return.

Will show at your convenience

(789) 123-4567

Figure 9.4   Rewrite of By-Owner Flyer.

immediate-response sales message. Whether it's a TV infomercial, or an 800 number in a magazine ad, advertisers load their sales messages with features and benefits. They try to persuade their target audience that their sales proposition offers the best value available.

Where to Distribute Your Flyers   Place the flyers in a waterproof tube or pouch and hang them on the for-sale sign that you place in the front yard of the property. In addition, distribute copies wherever you might reach targeted buyers:

- Neighborhood bulletin boards (such as those in grocery stores, libraries, and coffee shops)
- Neighborhood residents
- People you know at work, church, and clubs
- Neighborhood churches
- Mortgage companies and real estate firms
- Schools, colleges, and employers
- Homebuyer counseling agencies
- Apartment complexes (if you don't get thrown off the property)

Don't wait for buyers to find you. Bring your opportunity to them. At any given moment, many prospects for your property aren't actively searching. Rather, they're procrastinating. They're waiting for your sales message to push them off the dime. So hand out your flyers to anyone and everyone who might know of a potential buyer (or tenant).

Emphasize your $250 birddog fee.[1] I have bought and sold many properties through word of mouth. Unbelievably, few by-owner sellers or realty agents play this technique for all that it's worth.

Make Your Sign Stand Out

Use the largest for-sale sign that the law (or HOA rules) allows. On your for-sale sign, place as much appealing sales information as possible.

---

[1]Realtors have lobbied for laws that prohibit or restrict birddog fees. Check whether such restrictions apply in your area. If so, stay under the radar with your offer.

Similar to your flyer and classified ads, your for-sale sign must grab *A*ttention, create *I*nterest, generate *D*esire, and motivate passersby to *A*ction (AIDA). You want someone driving by at 40 miles per hour to recognize the great deal you offer.

> **Drivers must be able to read your sign without stopping their car.**

Sell with Honesty

Sales messages sell the sizzle, but you need to deliver the steak. You're entitled to tout the advantages of your property. No one's entitled to fabricate features that don't exist or cover up serious negatives that detract from the property. Go back to the agent flyer shown in Figure 9.2. By calling the property "beautiful," the agent-owner merely sets prospects up for disappointment. Had he advertised the property as a fixer (and priced it realistically), he would have sold it months before. When you misrepresent a property, you lose credibility, waste your time, and waste the time and efforts of homebuyers, tenants, and investors.

> **Extol virtues, don't try to fake it.**

Entrepreneurial renovators strive to give their buyers the best deal for the money. They do not try to dupe them into paying too much for too little. Establish credibility and potential buyers will come to you and ask, "When do you think that you'll have something else coming on stream? Please give us a call."

Sell the Property, Don't Just Show It

Your promotional efforts have worked their magic. The phone keeps ringing. You're about to "show" the property. Now what do you do? First, put your mind into reverse. Rewind and erase forever that thought that tells you to *show* the property. No, you are going to *sell it,* not

> **"Let me know if you have any questions" doesn't work as a sales presentation.**

show it. Selling a property demands a different perspective.

When people show properties, they assume a passive role. They let the buyer wander around and, if asked, they answer a question or two. When the prospect begins to leave, the passive showman says, "Thanks for coming by. Let me know if you think you might be interested."

In contrast, the active seller knows that prospects arrive full of hopes, fears, and uncertainties. The active seller *prepares* to address all of these buyer (tenant) concerns.

Prepare to Sell the Property

I looked at a for-sale-by-owner (FSBO) townhouse that was governed by a homeowners association. I asked the following questions:

Q.   May I see a copy of the resale package? I would like to check the CCRs.

A.   *What's a resale package? I don't know what you're referring to.*

Q.   Is there an attic?

A.   *Yes.*

Q.   Where can I get to it? I would like to see it.

A.   *The opening is in the laundry room ceiling.*

Q.   (After finding it) Do you have a stepladder I can use?

A.   *No. We don't have one.*

Q.   Do you know if homeowner association rules or zoning would permit me to finish off the attic?

A.   *No. Why would you want to do that? You would have to crawl up through that hole to get to it. (I then told her that you can buy a circular steel stairwell that's manufactured precisely for this purpose.)*

Q.   What's the status of that wooded area? (The townhouse property line abutted a large wooded tract of land.)

A.   *I don't know who owns that land or what they're going to do with it.*

Q.   Do you have an FHA or VA mortgage on the property?

A.   *FHA.*

Q.   How old is it and what's your rate?

A.   *Three years. Around eight-and-a-quarter percent, I think.*

Q.   Eight-and-a-quarter percent! Why haven't you refinanced? (FHA offers a streamlined refi that makes it easy and very cost effective to refi if rates drop by even 1 percent. At that time, 30-year fixed rates were at 6 percent.)

A.   *Our loan's only three years old. I think it would only save us about fifty dollars a month.*

> **Prepare to answer the questions that buyers *should* ask.**

Our conversation went on in the same vein. Neither she nor her husband (who was in a back bedroom getting ready for work) seemed to know anything about the property that a smart and informed buyer would want to learn. Indeed, although evidently unknown to the sellers, the financing issue was especially critical. Their FHA loan could have proved to be a powerful selling point. Owner-occupant buyers (but not investors) can assume the sellers' FHA mortgage at the same interest rate that the sellers are paying. Had these sellers streamlined an FHA refinance at 6 percent, a buyer could have stepped into the property and the mortgage for just a few thousand dollars out of pocket. However, at 8¼ percent, the assumption wouldn't look attractive to most buyers (because most buyers wouldn't know that they, too, could streamline the refi once their names went on the mortgage).

These sellers had elected the FSBO route because they had not accumulated enough equity in their property to pay the 6 or 7 percent Realtor sales commission. But no one buys from an FSBO just to help him avoid paying a Realtor fee. All buyers want and seek reasons to buy.

Not an Isolated Case

I do not mean to indict these hapless souls for their lack of salesmanship. They represent the norm. Sellers and real estate agents alike routinely confuse showing a property with *selling* a property. As a result, they become adept at announcing rooms—"This is the kitchen. Here's the den. The master bedroom's at the end of the hall"—but they fail to make the sale.

They do not realize that (except in hot markets) sellers must give prospects reasons to buy. Sellers must anticipate and address the prospects' fears and hopes. Sellers must move to close the sale now rather than later.

Sales Success: Your 12-Step Program

To move past showing and on to selling, follow these 12 steps to a successful sale.

> This 12-step program will convert lookers into buyers.

1. Back Up Your Sizzle with Facts   Collect data on comps. Photocopy pertinent regulatory ordinances. Provide a home warranty. Show school rankings. Map out the convenience of the location to important linkages (employers, shopping, culture, nightlife, parks, schools). Whatever selling points you want to make, secure documentary proof or persuasive evidence. Otherwise, you're just puffing.

2. Establish Rapport   Find common ground for chitchat. Before you extol kitchens and closets, find out about their kids, cars, or hobbies. "I see you're wearing a Notre Dame sweatshirt. Is that where you went to college?" "Really, you did? My son's a junior there now. . . ."

3. Segue into Likes and Dislikes   Never begin talking features and benefits until you've learned the prospects' hot buttons and turnoffs. "What would you like to see first? What features prompted your call? Would you like . . . ?" Too often sellers and realty agents launch into a monologue about features that the prospects care little about. Or even worse, they tout a feature the prospects find unappealing, thus driving buyers into a socially distant position. Out goes your rapport.

4. Diplomatically Discover Their Feelings about Other Properties They've Shopped   You think that you're offering a great property at a competitive price. But what do your prospects think? Ask for feedback about the market from the only people who really count—your potential buyers (renters).

5. Really Listen to the Criticism That Prospects Give You   You've worked hard to renovate the property to beat the competition. But, hey, none of us is perfect. Maybe you overlooked something. Ask your prospects for objections and weak points. Until you get a signed contract, keep searching for profit-enhancing improvements.

6. Translate Features into Motivating Benefits   Your prospects won't necessarily see the meaning of R-38 insulation, thermo-pane windows, a southern exposure, or R-1B zoning. Translate these features into benefits. "This heavy-grade insulation means that your heat and air costs will run less than $100 a month. Once this zoisha grass matures, your yard will look like a putting green and you'll never have to contend with crabgrass or weeds. Look at this photo. That's how the yard will look by the end of summer."

7. Inform the Prospects about Financing   First-time buyers, especially, may know little about down payments, monthly payments, and

> **Seek feedback.
> Don't give a
> monologue.**

closing costs. They may not realize that they can buy your property with only a few thousand cash out of pocket (which may be borrowed from relatives). They may not realize that their after-tax monthly house payments might cost them less than rent.

8. Monitor the Prospects' Emotional Responses and Body Language   Are they mentally moving their furniture into the home? Are they working through the financials in the context of their budget? Are they voicing seriously considered objections about price, terms, features, or neighborhood? Intensity of interest both positive and negative signals that they want to buy—if you alleviate their concerns and strengthen the facts and evidence that support your assurances.

> **Ask your
> prospects to
> buy (rent).**

9. Make It Easy to Close the Sale   Prepare your paperwork ahead of time. When you detect or elicit buy signals, move to the kitchen table (or sofa and coffee table) that you've brought into the house. If the prospects hesitate to commit, give more assurances along with the reasons why they really need to act now and not let this great property go to someone else. If necessary, agree to include short-term contingencies. However, retain the right to accept backup offers. If such an offer does come in, agree to give the original buyers 24 hours (possibly longer) to clear their contingency or lose their chance to own the property.

10. Set Up an Earnest Money Escrow   To seal the deal, ask the buyers to put up an earnest money deposit. If they're smart, they won't make out this check directly to you. Prearrange an escrow account with a title company (or other escrow agent). The buyers can then write the check directly to the escrow account. This technique gives the buyers more assurance that you're playing straight with them.

11. Follow Up a Successful Close   When you successfully close your buyers, follow up to achieve two goals: (1) Make sure they proceed quickly

> **You can't merely coast to closing. Remain alert for potholes in the road.**

to satisfy their contingencies (property inspection, mortgage approval, lawyer consultation); and (2) keep them motivated.

Some prospects suffer buyers' remorse. They begin to doubt their decision. You treat this disease with periodic positive updates. "A property down the street just sold for $10,000 more than you paid. The neighborhood elementary school has won an award for outstanding extracurricular programs. The city has pledged $500,000 to upgrade neighborhood streets and parks."

After buyers sign, assure them that they've made the right decision. Bolster their excitement and alleviate their regret and worry.

> **Prospects who are "just looking" today may become your buyers tomorrow.**

12. Follow Up an Unsuccessful Close When you first set up an appointment to sell the property, get the full names of the prospects and their telephone numbers. If you meet prospects through an open house that you're holding, ask visitors to register (name and phone number) for a door-prize drawing. Or when convenient, ask directly for their names and numbers (or business cards) and then enter them into a prospect register.

Learn who your prospects are and how to contact them. Then follow up with a thank-you note and additional persuasive information about the property. Many FSBOs let uncommitted prospects walk out the door with no plan to follow up. Ignite interest, desire, and action with periodic updates about the property, the availability of lower-rate financing, or other potentially motivating developments.

More Tips on Financing

The townhouse FSBOs failed to tell me about their assumable FHA financing. Even after I brought up the subject, these FSBOs never volunteered information about the amount of outstanding balance on their mortgage or used its assumability as a selling point. To see the importance of this failure, contrast the classified ad they ran with my rewrite using actual facts that I discovered through my sustained inquiries and investigations:

Original Owner Ad

3BR, 2BA, 1,600 sq. ft., huge master BR. On golf course, stone fireplace, cul-de-sac, $83,500. 555-1234, apt.

My Rewrite

Easy qualify. 3BR, 2BA, 1,600 sq. ft. low-maintenance, top-condition patio home. Quiet cul-de-sac bordering wooded tract. Large attic storage (den/BR/study conversion possible). Priced at only $85,500. $4,800 cash-to-close, $489 per month. 2144 Park Lane. Open Sat. & Sun. 12-5. 555-1234.

First, you may wonder why I removed "on golf course" and "huge master" from their ad. I did it because neither was true![2] Also, the ad appeared in the "Houses for Sale" category, but it was not a single-family house. It was a common-wall patio home. Again, the ad was misleading. My rewrite not only accented the terrific financing (i.e., if the owners had refinanced at 6 percent)—it substituted true positives for deceptive wording.

Avoid Deception

Let's go off point a bit here. The original seller's ad pushes me to again warn against using exaggerated and deceptive ads. Such ads only set up your prospects for letdown. Sure, "on golf course" makes the phone

---

[2]The golf course was actually behind the houses across the street from this property. And at 15 feet by 15 feet, the master bedroom can hardly qualify as "huge."

| Misleading ads turn off potential buyers. |

ring. But to what avail? As it was written, the ad targeted the wrong prospects and it failed to attract the people who would most value the features and affordability of the actual property.

Back to Financing

To successfully sell properties (especially to first-time buyers), plan ahead for financing. To make buying easier, offer your buyers owner financing or owner-assisted financing. Such financing includes, for example, seller seconds, contract-for-deed, lease option, and lease pur-

| Help your prospects "own," not just "buy." |

chase. Or you could put an assumable mortgage on the property when you buy it and then pass that financing along to your buyers. (We discuss these possibilities in Chapter 10.)

Cooperate with mortgage lenders. Let them write flyers that explain the down payment and monthly payment possibilities of the mortgage plans they offer. Then use these handouts to show buyers how little cash and income they will need to *own* your property. Although some prospects will obtain a mortgage preapproval, others will not. To make a sale, make financing easy.

(Note: When you talk with prospects, use the word *own* rather than *buy*—as in "You can *own* this great house for just $15,000 cash to close and $1,600 a month. Given these figures, doesn't *owning* look a lot better than wasting money on rent?")

Should You Employ a Realty Agent?

Most owners who try to sell their own properties fail. They put out their cardboard front-yard sign, run a newspaper ad for a month or two,

> **Most FSBOs fail to realize that sales agents provide a wide range of services for sellers.**

and then give up. Do these failures mean that you should forget FSBO and list your property with a realty agent? Not at all; but it does mean that to succeed where others fail, you must avoid their mistakes.

Most FSBOs do not realize that to sell properties, *top* sales agents go far beyond yard signs and newspaper ads. To get properties sold, top agents provide services to sellers and buyers.

Services to Sellers

1. *24/7.* Agents work whenever they get called, and they remain on call morning, noon, and night every day of the week.

   Advice for FSBO sellers: Make yourself available to show the property on a moment's notice at nearly any waking hour.

2. *Multiple media.* Agents use yard signs and newspaper ads, but they rely on referrals, networking, web sites, cold calling, floor time, and personal and business relationships.

   Advice for FSBO sellers: Get the word out about your property to everyone you know or come in contact with. Circulate those flyers.

3. *Pricing.* Agents inspect and show dozens of properties every week. They know properties, and they know the details of purchase contracts.

   Advice for FSBO sellers: Look at properties in the neighborhood and nearby areas. Monitor sales prices, terms, and time on market. Price the property realistically in the context of other transactions.

4. *Home preparation.* Agents obtain feedback about properties from dozens of buyers each month. They learn the likes and dislikes of the market. They can use this knowledge to help sellers dress their house for success.

   Advice for FSBO sellers: Monitor buyer feedback. Talk with realty agents, contractors, home remodelers, and sales consultants at home improvement centers. Give buyers what they really want.

5. *Sales presentations.* Top agents don't show properties, they sell them. They know how to encourage buy signals. They know how to alleviate buyer objections. They diplomatically buffer hard-edged negotiations and persistently create trade-offs, options, and alternatives. They maintain a supply of purchase agreements. They know how to get buyers to commit and sign.

    Advice for FSBO sellers: Encourage your prospects and ask them to buy. Shy and passive won't make it. Remain flexible and open to offers. Give and take with tact and good nature. Persuasively lead your prospects into a buying decision. Don't wait for them to ask you.

6. *Troubleshoot problems.* Agents know that signed contracts don't close themselves. Someone must monitor the flow of paperwork and solve problems that can throw a sale off course.

    Advice for FSBO sellers: Don't assume that you can walk the path from contract to closing without hitting a few potholes. Monitor the flow. Rely on a careful escrow agent to diligently control the document shuffle.

Services to Buyers

1. *Market knowledge.* Agents know listings and can prescreen properties to save the buyers' effort.

    Advice for FSBO sellers: Be able to compare and contrast your property with others on the market. Especially highlight its competitive advantages.

2. *Agents help buyers with neighborhood selection.* People don't just buy houses, they buy locations. Agents know demographics, schools, trends, commuting distances, shopping, and culture. Buyers depend on agents to compare and contrast the pros and cons of neighborhoods.

    Homebuyers rely on their agents for many services.

    Advice for FSBO sellers: Understand the neighborhood. Know how it compares to others. What

are its advantages? Prepare a neighborhood flyer to complement the flyer you've prepared for the property itself. Homebuyers who are new to a city especially need this information.

3. *Price.* Buyers depend on agents to advise about price. In turn,
   agents provide buyers comp sales data. Agents also help buyers
   choose their offering price.

   Advice for FSBO sellers: Provide prospects with comp
   sales data. Emphasize how your price, terms, and property features beat those offered by the competition. Do not push prospects to learn these facts on their own. Other owners (and their
   agents) will spin facts to their own advantage—not yours.

4. *Financing.* Agents either qualify buyers or refer them to a loan
   rep who provides this service. First-time buyers need someone
   to figure out how much home they can afford and the quality
   of their credit profile.

   Advice for FSBO sellers: Establish a relationship with several loan reps. Discuss the features and costs of loan programs
   with prospects. Refer prospects to www.myfico.com, where
   for around $39.95 they can look at three credit reports, learn
   their FICO (Fair Isaacs Company) credit scores, and gain tips
   on how to improve their credit profile. Even better, help the
   buyers with owner-assisted financing or a mortgage assumption (Chapter 10).

5. *Negotiating assistance.* Many buyers, and especially first-time
   buyers, do not feel comfortable or competent in the negotiating process. In their role as facilitator and mediator, agents
   ease their buyers through the offer-counteroffer emotional
   roller coaster.

   Advice for FSBO sellers: Play softball, not hardball.
   Contemplate and conciliate. Help prospects feel comfortable
   in talking with you. Nurture trust. "Let's see if we can work
   out an agreement that will make us all happy," not, "Look, take
   it or leave it. If you don't want the property, I'm sure someone
   else will."

6. *Follow through.* Agents help buyers follow through to submit
   their mortgage application and obtain a professional inspection

of the property. They may also hand hold and troubleshoot for the buyers. The agent remains on call to provide assurances and intervene when an obstacle arises (low appraisal, mortgage turndown, encroachments, etc.).

Advice for FSBO sellers: Your agent can assist with some of these details. But tell the buyers that they can call you at any time to assist with problems or answer questions about the property, the neighborhood, the mortgage loan process, or anything else that concerns them. Provide the buyers with the names of respected property inspectors, pest control companies (for termite clearance), and surveyors (if necessary).

I have repeated myself throughout this chapter, and I have done so because I want you to succeed as an FSBO seller. If you follow the renovation and marketing process that we've gone through, you can outperform most agents. You will earn a higher profit, give your buyers a better deal, sell quicker, or achieve some combination of each.

> **FSBOs "save the commission" only when they market their properties effectively.**

"Saving the commission" usually requires planning and effort. If you prefer not to replicate the services that top realty agents provide, that's fine. Try the easy route that most FSBOs follow. Put up a sign, run an ad, and hope a preapproved buyer shows up with a checkbook in one hand and a written, full-asking-price offer in the other.

It does happen. And with a great property to sell, your chances of such success go up. But (except in hot markets), experience teaches us to go beyond the ordinary. Selling real estate seldom counts as the "lazy man's way to riches."

Co-op Sales

If working alone as an FSBO seller doesn't appeal to you, offer sales agents a 3 percent (more or less) commission to bring you a buyer. You act as your own listing agent and pay the co-op percentage to the buyer's agent. With this approach, you increase the chance of a sale, but if you find the buyer yourself, you owe the agents nothing.

Try a co-op deal.	Indeed, as soon as your FSBO sign goes up, agents will flood you with telephone calls. Many of these agents don't care much about selling property. They want to list it. To reach *selling* agents, try

distributing your flyers in real estate offices.

What about Lawyers?

Fortunately, the majority of my small residential real estate transactions have occurred lawyer free. In those transactions where lawyers have been involved, the lawyers created more expense and trouble than they were worth. In fact, I do not know any real estate investor who has much good to say about lawyers.

Lawyers can hinder as well as help.	Nevertheless, it's becoming ever more difficult to safely remain in a lawyer-free zone. (And in some areas, such as New York City, lawyers routinely represent buyers even in simple home-buying transactions. Lawyers in Maryland lobbied the state legislature for a statute that would force all homebuyers to employ a lawyer—whether they

wanted one or not.)

So, when you do choose to employ an attorney to draft your sales (or purchase) agreement or advise on other matters, beware. It's tough to find a competent, trustworthy lawyer who does not overbill and/or underperform. Many lawyers, too, like to voice their opinions about property investments even when such knowledge lies outside their area of expertise.

As you progress as a real estate investor, the increasing complexity of land use, fair housing, landlord-tenant, income tax, and environmental laws—to name just a few issues of concern—will require you to enlist legal counsel. Avoid searching the Yellow Pages. Solicit attorney s from experienced property investors. Verify specialized expertise in the areas of law that directly relate to your immediate concerns. (For example, a landlord-tenant lawyer probably knows little about zoning. An attorney who writes contracts may prove quite inadequate on matters of taxation.)

10

Buy Your Property

You have explored many possibilities for creating value in real estate and then successfully marketing the product you've created. Now, you're going to discover where to find your fix-and-flip properties and how to negotiate good deals.

Find Good Properties

Where can you find good properties? Here are the leading sources:

- ◆ Real estate agents
- ◆ Newspapers
- ◆ Tour neighborhoods
- ◆ Networking
- ◆ Foreclosures and REOs
- ◆ The Internet

Real Estate Agents

In most metro areas, real estate agents list about 60 percent of the properties that are available for sale. Another 20 percent consist of FSBOs (for sale by owners), and the remaining 20 percent include three other

> **You can often buy properties that aren't listed or advertised for sale.**

sources: property owners who are willing to sell but are not actively marketing their properties, foreclosures, and REOs (real estate owned; primarily foreclosed real estate that is now owned by banks, other types of mortgage lenders, and government agencies).

Advantages of Working with Agents Relatively few investors go it alone in their search for properties. Even though investors don't need the hand-holding service that agents provide first-time homebuyers, investors do value four services:

1. *Screening properties.* Every day, new listings come onto the market, old listings expire, some listings cut their prices, and some properties get sold. Good agents will monitor these market activities. They will alert their preferred investors of all market developments that those investors could turn to their advantage.
2. *Saving the investors' time.* In screening properties and property transactions, agents not only alert investors to emerging opportunities but also save them enormous amounts of time and effort.
3. *Negotiating savvy.* Top agents can help investors craft their deals. They know how to present offers, create alternatives, and get transactions closed.
4. *Sources of money.* Top agents not only stay abreast of the institutional mortgage market—they also can uncover little-known sources of funding.

If you choose to work with an agent, expect at least these four services. To gain the most benefit, discuss what you're looking for, the types of financing that you would like, and how frequently you want the agent to contact you. For preferred service, buy from one favored agent—but only for so long as that agent fulfills the services and gathers the information that you request. Quid pro quo rules.

> **Your agent can screen properties that meet your criteria.**

Disadvantages of Agents   A real estate agent creates negatives as well as positives:

1. *High fees.* Most sellers pay a sales commission of 4 to 7 percent of the selling price of a property. Absent these fees, you and the seller could "split the savings" and both come out ahead. The sales commission looms especially large when you try to negotiate a bargain price with a low-equity seller.

2. *Conflict of interest.* Agents get paid when their sales close. Some agents will try to talk you into a bad deal to earn the commission. Until you build a relationship of trust with an agent, critically eye all advice. Weigh, consider, and verify.

3. *Too little knowledge.* From this book you will learn more about neighborhood and property analysis than a majority of sales agents. You may need to weed through substantial incompetence before you match up with an agent who fulfills your legitimate expectations.

> **Insist on an agent who knows how to work intelligently.**

Many sales agents think of their job as a numbers game. Talk to a lot of people, hand out 1,000 business cards a month, chauffeur prospects around, and *show* properties. Eventually someone lists or buys something. Most sales agents (and FSBOs) do not realize that selling requires service, knowledge, and integrity. When you find an agent who demonstrates those virtues, you've found someone who might earn those high fees.

Newspapers

When novice investors think about using the newspaper to help search for properties, they needlessly restrict themselves to the Houses for Sale section of the classifieds and the realtor display ads. But you can use the newspaper to discover properties in many other ways.

> **Read current and past FSBO ads.**

For-Sale-by-Owner Ads   I have found more of my small residential properties from by-owner ads than via any other source. Although some investors prefer to work through agents, I prefer going direct. Usually, you can find your best low-down-payment, owner-will-carry (OWC) sellers in the FSBO ads. In addition to calling current ads, I periodically call ads from 30 to 90 days back. If the sellers haven't sold (and haven't listed with an agent), I often find them more open to offer. If a sale has occurred, I try to extract as much information as I can to strengthen my knowledge of the market.

I telephone ads primarily on the basis of price and location. Many ads lack sufficient content, so I don't rule out properties based on omissions. You score your best bargains when you see possibilities and hidden values that the owner (or agent) misses.

> **Realtor ads intentionally leave out important information.**

Realtor Newspaper Ads   Realtors place their ads to generate phone calls. They want you to call so they can ask you what you're looking for and then try to set up an appointment to show you several other properties. That's okay if you're not currently working with an agent. If you are, then don't call the ad. Call your agent and ask him or her what they know about the property and whether it's likely to fit the property profile that you've specified.

> **Lease options give you a low-cost way to control a property.**

Lease Option   We discuss lease options in Chapter 12. For now, call about every lease option property that comes on the market in your targeted price range and neighborhood(s). Lease options give the ultimate low-cost method to control a property while you complete fix-up and renovations. Write an assignability clause into your option agreement that permits you to achieve a low-cost exit strategy.

House-for-Rent Ads   Many property owners become accidental landlords or tired landlords. Even when owners are

> **Landlords are often would-be sellers. Ask them.**

committed investors, they may be open to offers. If a rental house looks like it holds good promise, I'll ask the owners if they're interested in either a sale or a lease option. Given that these owners originally sought to rent the property, they're not counting on a huge inflow of cash. Their financial situation can easily permit them to offer flexible, low cash-up-front terms. Persuade them to do so.

Wanted to Buy   Some investors use the Wanted to Buy section of the classified ads to locate distressed owners in hopes of snagging a bargain. Their ad might read something like this:

> I buy houses for cash. End your hassles with agents and tire kickers. Money in your hand within 72 hours. All offers considered. Please call Tom anytime. (888) 888-1234.

Several ads such as this one run continuously in our local paper. The ads must work or someone is wasting money. I've never used the quick-cash gambit but have succeeded many times with an ad such as the following:

> Experienced investor with cash, credit, and references seeks owner-financed houses and income properties. Please call Dr. Eldred, (888) 123-4567.

Or when I was just starting out, a wanted-to-buy ad similar to the following paid off for me with more replies than I could handle:

> Ambitious young investor would like to acquire rental properties. Owner financing preferred. Strong references. You enjoy the interest income, I'll do the work. Please call Gary, (888) 123-4567.

If you run a wanted-to-buy ad, include a personal element with some indicator of credibility. In a world where the number of retirees

> **Find clues and leads throughout the newspaper.**

is increasing and after-tax CD rates and dividend yields from stocks fail to match the rate of inflation, we'll see more owners who will sell OWC to someone they perceive as low risk. In today's market, OWC interest income provides a high yield relative to alternatives.

Public Notices and Community News   Each day people marry, divorce, or experience financial setbacks such as lawsuits, foreclosures, and job losses due to business failure, company downsizing, or plant closure. In addition, people die. Newspapers duly report all of these life-changing events. What do these events mean to you? They could signal that someone may need to sell a less-than-perfect house relatively quickly.

That's why some hustling real estate agents rely on local news and public notices to provide a fruitful source of potential sellers and buyers. You can do the same. Talk with some of these people before an agent gets their listing. You'll often score a good deal.

Which Newspapers?   Up to this point, I've talked about "the" newspaper. But unless you live in a small town, your area probably supports anywhere from 3 to 10 newspapers. In addition to the standard local paper(s) that carry the city's name, you might consult real estate ads in the newspaper(s) published by the local college(s), want-ad-type papers such as the *Thrifty Nickel,* and newspapers that circulate in distinct communities where you might like to buy (e.g., in San Diego, the *La Jolla Light*; in Sarasota, the *Pelican* and the *Longboat Key Observer;* and in Oakland, the *Montclarian*). Given the high advertising cost of major dailies, the smaller-circulation papers often provide highly targeted, cost-effective leads.

I know a condominium developer in suburban Chicago who went broke buying display ads for his project in the *Chicago Tribune.* The investor who took over the development switched to advertising in the suburban paper that reached thousands of nearby apartment dwellers. This investor sold the condo project in four months. Target marketing works.

Drive, Bike, or Run Neighborhoods

> **Get out of your car.**

Get out and regularly bike (or run as I do) your targeted neighborhoods. Drive if you must, but you'll discover much more when you're out of your car and you don't have to worry about slowing down traffic each time you hit the brakes to glimpse a better view of a promising property.

For-Sale Signs   In touring neighborhoods, try to spot for-sale signs. Also take note of for-rent signs and all property flyers. Your search process doesn't just alert you to properties you may want to buy. It also tells you what's selling and renting and at what prices and rent levels. If you notice available properties that aren't moving, investigate why.

> **Get firsthand information.**

When you see neighbors, tenants, or sellers of promising properties, strike up an informal conversation. Gain insights that might not be as easy to come by in a formal purchase visit to the property. Neighbors and tenants can be especially forthcoming in a way that helps inform my negotiating strategy. "Why are they selling?" you might ask. "How long has the property been on the market? Do you know if the owners need or want a quick sale?" You're looking for all types of information that will help you size up the situation.

Verrry Interesting   As you talk with neighborhood residents and tour an area, tune your hearing and sharpen your vision to pick up on such things as:

- Changes for good or bad that may affect future property values
- People who plan to sell within the next 12 months
- Properties that appear neglected, or even better, vacant or abandoned
- Properties that display hidden value potential (conversion, oversized or double lot, rightsizing)

The more knowledge you gain, the quicker you can judge a property when opportunities present themselves. Likewise, with knowledge, you create your own possibilities.

Networking

Just as networking can help you sell a property, it can help you locate a good property to buy. Tell everyone you know that you're in the market and the kinds of deals that you will consider. Networking offers more possibilities than most investors realize.

> **Nearly everyone's a buyer or seller at some time. Ask them.**

Most property owners prefer a quick, certain, and no-hassle sale at a lower price. If they list with a realty firm, they must not only pay a 4 to 7 percent sales commission but also place their house and their lives on display for a period of months. Use these facts to persuade owners to sell to you at market value *less* the amount of the sales commission and some further discount (say 2 to 5 percent) for fast, convenient, and easy.

Foreclosures and REOs

The foreclosure process offers four shots to bag a bargain price:

- ◆ Preforeclosure workout
- ◆ Foreclosure auction
- ◆ Immediate postforeclosure purchase
- ◆ Lender REO

Preforeclosure Workout   When property owners fall behind on their mortgage payments, the lender either threatens to sic its lawyers on them (iron fist approach) or pleads with the borrowers to come in, sit down, and schedule a payment catch-up or sell the property voluntarily (velvet glove approach). Previously, lenders relied on the iron fists of their lawyers to beat delinquent borrowers into submission. Today, many lenders have wised up and cover those fists with a velvet glove that's holding an olive branch.

Your Role   Because lenders favor a loan workout over foreclosure, investors sometimes step in to stop the growing losses of both the borrowers and the lender. Offer the defaulting owners some walkaway money. Offer the lender something less than the defaulting borrowers are legally obligated to pay, but something more than the lender would *net* from a foreclosure sale. Or, if the potential of the property warrants, assume the full obligations of the borrowers. In exchange, ask the lender for a reduced interest rate, an additional advance of renovation money, or other concessions in the costs or terms of financing.

When borrowers stand little chance of holding onto their house, lenders usually try to minimize their loses in lieu of chasing after dollars that they will never recover.

> **Workouts require tact and perseverance.**

Show Empathy, Credibility, and Diplomacy   Once the foreclosure filing notice hits the newspaper, the foreclosure vultures will descend on the defaulting borrowers to scavenge what remains of their home equity and self-dignity. To succeed against vultures, show empathy, credibility, and diplomacy.

Empathy means that you sincerely tailor a solution that permits the borrowers to salvage their credit record, home equity, and self-esteem. Credibility means that you prove to the borrowers that you're not just whistling *Dixie*. Prove to them that you can come up with the cash or credit to quickly close a deal. Diplomacy means that you listen more than you talk, that you search for a win-win-win outcome, and that you're not just another "Take it or leave it" profit monger.

The Foreclosure Sale   When defaulting borrowers ignore their chance for workout (as they often do), the county sheriff (or other appointed officer of the law) sells the property to the highest bidder at a foreclosure sale. Such sales seldom bring in enough to clear the balance on the

> **Foreclosure sales typically go to risk-taking speculators or the foreclosing lender.**

mortgage, other liens, legal expenses, and unpaid property taxes. In fact, the foreclosure auctions seem designed to sell at the lowest possible price.

Winning bidders do not receive a warranty deed to the property. They receive no disclosures about property defects. They receive no assurance of possession. (The buyer at a foreclosure auction may need to evict the existing tenants or owners of the property.) Winning bidders must pay cash for the property, and their bid must not include any contingencies (such as a property inspection, termite clearance, environmental clearance, or lawyer approval).

Given these risks, the foreclosure sale attracts only two types of buyers: (1) foreclosure speculators, and (2) the lender who is foreclosing the mortgage. Contrary to the hype of foreclosure gurus who deceptively peddle their books, tapes, and seminars, beginning investors can rarely play the foreclosure game without incurring risks.

Immediate Postforeclosure   However, after the auction gavel comes down, beginning investors can safely spring into action. For regardless of whether the winning bid comes from a foreclosure speculator or the mortgage lender, neither of these buyers typically plans to hold that property as a long-term investment. Both prefer to exit quickly. The speculator wants to turn the property for a quick profit. The lender wants to clear its books of this nonperforming asset.

> **Buy from the winner of the foreclosure sale.**

Here's how you might work this situation to your advantage. Offer the winning bidder something more than the amount she has paid at the foreclosure auction, but something less than the "as-is" market value of the property. But condition your offer with a financing contingency, various inspections, and title insurance—all of which you should be able to satisfy within a week or two. If (when) everything checks out satisfactorily, the winning bidder enjoys a quick, easy, and profitable sale. You obtain a bargain price for the property without the risks of buying at foreclosure.

Shop the REOs   When lenders end up with a foreclosure, that property goes onto their books as an REO (real estate owned).

HUD/VA, Fannie, and Freddie   If the mortgage loan on that property was owned by Freddie Mac or Fannie Mae or backed up by the Department of Veterans Affairs (VA) or the Federal Housing Administration (HUD/FHA), the company or government agency will step in and take the property. Then that company (or agency) puts the house up for sale and markets it according to its rules and procedures.

Contrary to what some authors lead you to believe, Fannie, Freddie, HUD, and VA nearly always price their REO properties at (or close to) market value. Typically, you can score great deals with their properties only in periods of severe market distress or when the REO owner wants to dump a distressed property (which involves risks for the buyer). My book, *Investing in Real Estate* (5th ed., Wiley, 2005), devotes a chapter to the REO policies of Fannie, Freddie, HUD, and VA. It pays to stay abreast of these types of REOs, but don't believe the hype. It's usually difficult to pick up these (or any other) REOs for dimes on the dollar.

> **Lenders usually list their REOs with realty firms.**

Lender-Held REOs   When a lender takes back an REO, it usually lists the property with a local realty firm. So, monitor the foreclosure auction and immediately contact the foreclosing lender before it places the property with an agent. In a quid-pro-quo world, many mortgage lenders who count on referrals for their mortgage business from realty agents won't deal with investors directly. If you need to work through an agent, you still might negotiate a good deal on a lender-held REO.

Every REO lender is open to offers. The longer they own the property, the more money they lose in maintenance, upkeep, security costs to ward off vandals, and lost interest earnings. Plus, lenders who end up with nonperforming assets on their books look bad to shareholders and regulators. Sooner or later, most lenders become motivated sellers. At that point, the lender may cut a deal on price, terms, interest rate, or some combination of the three. Also, as you concede on some issues, you might propose that the lender advance you funds for renovations.

How do you know when the lender intends to move on a deal? You don't. To win with lender REOs, persist. Stay in touch. Keep offers coming in. I know of instances where a lender has turned down, say, $400,000, and three months later accepted $300,000. Persistence pays off.

The World Wide Web

Every method of finding properties has its web site counterpart(s). The web devotes sites to realty firms, MLS listings, FSBOs, foreclosures, and REOs. Network through investor groups and chat rooms. Search newspaper classified ads without ever buying a newspaper.

> **Turn up your best information through personal contacts.**

Through Mapquest.com you can pinpoint the location of a property with directions on how best to get there. To learn about comp sales in the neighborhood, school rankings, or crime rates, there are a dozen web sites that will give you this information. On some sites, you can even experience a virtual tour of the property. To learn sales prices, go to your county assessor's web site or zillow.com.

Nevertheless, even though you might turn to the web for preliminary information, nothing beats touring neighborhoods, collecting facts from firsthand conversations, and talking with property owners, agents, sellers, and tenants. The axiom rings true: "Real estate's not about property, it's about people." Use the Web to begin or expand your property search and fact checking. But your best information will be delivered to you personally.

Search for Agreement

Many inexperienced investors approach purchase negotiations with uncertainty. They don't quite know what to expect. Some falsely

> It takes two
> willing parties
> to structure an
> agreement.

believe, too, that a skillful negotiator dips into a bag of tricks and pulls out deceptive techniques like lowballing, weasel clauses (contingencies written primarily as easy escape hatches), running a bluff, shotgunning (multiple random offers), "dressing to impress" (pretending to be something you're not), bad-mouthing (deflating the owners' high opinion of their home), asking for the moon and the stars, and eleventh-hour surprises (at the last minute before closing, insisting on contract changes in your favor). One book on real estate negotiating even advises, "Remember you are in a war and must use every weapon available to win."

These hardball tactics make sense to those who use them, but experience shows that they often backfire. Successful investors don't seek to win the negotiation. They negotiate to win an *agreement* that will actually close to the benefit of all parties. "The tendency of many sellers," says Realtor Bill Sloan, "is for them to stop listening if the purchase price offer is too low."

> Working "with"
> creates more
> deals than
> working
> "against."

Sloan points out a well-known fact: To most sellers, price stands out as the main event. Everything else is warm-up. That's why lowball offers knock negotiations off the track before they even get going.

When you realize this fact, however, you can use it to your advantage. By not pushing the sellers too hard on price, you may get most everything else you want. Or if you really put bargain price at the top of your negotiating list, prepare to give the sellers enough other points to persuade them that your proposal makes sense from their perspective.

> Look for high-
> value/low-value
> deal points and
> trade-offs.

Deal Points

Besides price, purchase negotiations will include at least 10 deal points, such as the following:

1. *Terms.* Will the seller offer owner-assisted financing? If so, how much up-front cash? What interest rate? What amount of monthly payments? What type of assistance (lease option, lease purchase, land contract, first mortgage, second mortgage, etc.)?

2. *Closing costs.* In most areas, custom dictates who pays what settlement expenses. But negotiation overrides custom. With settlement costs often amounting to $5,000 or more, smart investors put these amounts on the table for discussion.

3. *Earnest money deposit.* To show your commitment to a deal, bind your offer with an earnest money deposit. How much should that be? That's negotiable.

4. *Repair allowance.* In lieu of (or along with) a price reduction, you can negotiate a repair allowance for some of the fix-up work you plan for the property.

5. *Personal property.* Would you like the seller to include window air conditioners, appliances, or other personal property in the sale? Write them into your offer.

6. *Financing contingencies.* If the seller does not provide financing, include a financing contingency in your offer. This clause specifies the time to raise the money to close. It also sets the terms (interest rate, loan-to-value, down payment, etc.) that you must be able to obtain. Otherwise, you're released from the purchase agreement and entitled to a return of your earnest money.

7. *Inspection contingencies.* Get the property professionally inspected for physical condition, termites, and environmental hazards. How long to complete these inspections? Who pays how much for unanticipated or previously unknown problems? Under what scenarios can you withdraw from the agreement without obligation? Negotiation settles these issues.

8. *Closing date.* To gain a bargain price, many investors offer a fast closing. Does your seller voice a strong preference?

9. *Possession date.* Generally, sellers relinquish possession on or around the date of closing. Sometimes, though, you may want a delayed closing with early possession (such as with a

lease purchase or lease option). Or alternatively, the sellers may want to cash out fast, but remain in the property until, say, the school year ends or their new home is ready for them to move into.

10. *Warranties.* Is the seller providing you a home warranty or any specific warranties for components such as the roof, HVAC, or appliances? What exactly do the warranties cover, for what amounts, and for what period of time?

Every purchase-sale agreement addresses 10 or more major deal points. Negotiators never view any one of these issues as separate from the others. Instead, find a combination that works for everyone.

> **Work to find that right combination of deal points.**

Reduce Seller Anxiety

Often sellers will agree to accept a "pro-buyer" agreement—if you show them that you are a solid buyer and that the deal will actually close. To persuade sellers and reduce their anxiety, draw from the following eight negotiating tactics:

1. Increase the amount of your earnest money deposit.
2. Produce a preapproval letter from a mortgage lender or other assurances that you have the money and credit to do the deal.
3. If you're paying cash or making a large down payment, emphasize that fact. Cash counts. If you've got it, use it to boost the credibility of your position.
4. Emphasize the strength of your character, stability in your job and community, how you plan to improve the property, and other positive factors.
5. Avoid weasel clauses in your offer. A weasel clause lets you easily escape from (weasel out of), a contract without obligation. The most obvious weasel clauses states, "This offer is subject to the approval of my attorney." If you need to consult an attorney, do it before you begin negotiations. (In some states, by custom,

attorneys routinely negotiate property purchase agreements. Nevertheless, the same principle holds. Close your easy escape hatches and the sellers will accept more readily.

6. Avoid indefinite contingency clauses such as, "Offer subject to raising $50,000 from my business partners"; or sometimes homeowners write into their purchase offer, "Subject to the sale of our current home." Clauses like these raise the sellers' doubts, increase their anxiety, and generate resistance to your offer.

7. When you write a contingency clause into a contract, make it definite and short term. "Buyer will secure a property inspection report within five days," or "Buyer agrees to submit mortgage loan application within 48 hours," or "Sellers are released from obligation if buyers do not produce a letter of mortgage loan approval within three days." These clauses show that you are serious about closing the deal.

8. Write realistic contingency clauses. Don't expect to find mortgage money at 6 percent if market rates are at 7.5 percent. Research zoning and building regulations before you write your offer.

Submit your offer with no more contingencies than you need (but no fewer, either). Many sellers will lower their price for the peace of mind of a near-certain sale. That's why buyers who pay cash nearly always gain more seller concessions than those who load their contracts with ifs, ands, or buts.

Win-Win Isn't for Wimps

Negotiators typically fit into one of three negotiating categories: (1) adversarial, (2) accommodating, and (3) win-win. Lawyers typically practice the adversarial style. Adversarial negotiators make outrageous demands. They push, pull, or threaten to move you as close as possible to their position. Adversarial negotiators don't care whether their opponents end up pleased. All they care about is winning for themselves.

In contrast to the adversarial approach, the accommodating negotiator tends to give in to every request or demand. Accommodators feel
powerless to effect the outcome they want. They feel helpless due to
lack of money, time, information, knowledge, or experience. Accommodators detest conflict. They would rather lose than stand their ground.
When negotiating through a real estate agent or other third party, accommodators typically delegate too much responsibility. Accommodators often say things like, "Oh, just do what you think is best" or "Let's
just sign and get the whole thing over."

> **Think multiple
> directions, not
> a win-lose
> continuum.**

When you negotiate win-win, you adopt some
of the adversarial style and some of the accommodating style. But overall, you adopt a cooperative
perspective. Win-win negotiators recognize that
every negotiation brings forth multiple issues, priorities, and possibilities. They respect the other
party's (not opponent's) concerns, feelings, and
needs. They do not operate along a single line of
contention (e.g., price). Win-win negotiators work
to create a strong, mutually beneficial agreement that all parties want
to complete.

Yet, they never lie down in a fetal position while an adversary hurls
hardballs at them. When push comes to shove, win-win negotiators
either shove back to reestablish a cooperative enterprise or they walk
away with their dignity and finances intact.

Develop a Cooperative Attitude

Most importantly, win-win demands a cooperative approach. Bob Woolf,
agent, attorney, and past negotiator for many well-known figures including Larry Bird, Larry King, and Joe Montana, says, "When I enter a
negotiation, my attitude is, 'I'm going to make a deal.' I don't start with
a negative thought or word. I try to foster a spirit of cooperation. I want
the other party to feel that I'm forthright, cheerful, confident, and deter-
mined to reach their goals. If I'm sufficiently sensitive to the other party,
I firmly believe they will be predisposed to make an agreement with me.
To a degree, your attitude will become a self-fulfilling prophecy."

Bob Woolf's advice applies whether you negotiate a big-time sports contract or a purchase agreement for a property. In fact, especially with a purchase agreement for a home, you're wise to display a cooperative "Let's reach an agreement" attitude. Act in good faith. Play by the rules of courtesy. You want to buy a property. The sellers want to sell a property. You succeed when all parties cooperate to help each other.

Learn as Much as You Can about the Sellers

> To negotiate effectively, understand the sellers.

Some sales agents do everything they can to keep buyers and sellers away from each other—for good reason. Agents see sales fall through because personalities clash. Or they fear that sellers (since agents of yesteryear nearly always represented sellers) might give away a choice bit of information that will help the buyers.

"Why are you selling?" the buyers ask.

"Oh, Mack's been transferred," the sellers respond. "We have to be in Omaha by the end of next month."

Although the keep-the-buyers-and-sellers-apart sales strategy sometimes works best, as a rule I reject it. Before you make an offer, learn about the sellers. What kind of people are they? Do they seem generous and open? Are they rigid and argumentative? Do they show pride in their property? Are they reluctantly moving? Are they eager to leave? Why are they selling? Have they bought another home? What are their important needs: emotional, personal, and financial? What are their worries and concerns?

What Do the Sellers Really Want?   The sellers aren't really trying to sell a property. They're reaching for more distant goals. Selling their property provides a means to those ends. The sellers do not judge the price and terms of an offer by absolute standards. They judge it according to how well it helps them move toward what they want to achieve. So, get to know the sellers. Understand their needs; otherwise, you miss a great opportunity to find high-value/low-value win-win trade-offs that benefit both parties.

Say the sellers previously accepted two offers that fell through because the buyers couldn't arrange financing. With these experiences, the sellers may be anxious. They don't want to be strung out again. If you assure them that you have the resources to buy (bank statements, credit score, preapproval letter, job security), they will concede on price or other issues.

Establish Rapport and Emotional Connection   Frequently, investors and sellers aim their negotiating guns toward price. The sellers want a higher price. The buyers want a lower price. Push and pull dominate. Steer

> **Play it cool. Avoid clashes with the sellers.**

around this trap. Meet the sellers, talk with them, learn their perceptions, past selling experiences, feelings, and needs. But keep in mind that agent concerns about personality clashes are valid. When meeting and talking with sellers, follow these guidelines:

♦ *Meet the sellers as soon as possible.* The sooner you get a fix on who they are and what they're like, the better you can begin to map your negotiation strategy. Sellers respond more openly with information when you first look at their property. At that point they're eager to please. They want to excite your interest. If you wait to meet them until after you've made an offer, they'll guard their disclosures and concessions more tightly.

♦ *Get concessions before you begin to negotiate.* "You're asking $625,000, is that right? Just so I can fairly compare your property to others, have you thought about the price that would satisfy you?" Or: "You're asking $625,000. What personal property—appliances, drapes, rugs, patio furniture, gazebo, and so on—do you include?" Or maybe: "Have you considered how much financing you're willing to carry back?" By suggesting concessions in this way, you're not explicitly negotiating with the sellers. You're not even asking for concessions. You merely gather information to rank the sellers' property against other houses that are up for sale. Sensing that you will explore alternatives, most sellers will sweeten their deal before you write your offer.

◆ *Inquire, don't interrogate.* The way you ask questions is more important than the questions themselves. Phrase them as innocu-ously as you can. Don't intimidate, accuse, threaten, or debate. Maybe you've watched TV reruns of *Columbo*, the per-petually "disoriented" detective. Columbo didn't interrogate sus-pects. He gently probed. Use similar tactics. Encourage the easy flow of information. Don't extract it.

◆ *Establish rapport.* Find common ground. Talk about the last Cubs game, the weather, or perhaps a shared hobby. Negotia-tions are about people, not money. Treat the sellers as people, not merely owners of a property that you might want to buy.

◆ *Compliment, don't criticize.* As you inspect the property, find something nice to say. Note the sellers' grandfather clock. "Does it have an interesting history? How long have you owned it?" Comment on belongings they take pride in. What about the yard? Do the sellers have a green thumb? Can you admire their tomatoes or roses?

At this *first* meeting, express a cordial attitude. Establish a *relationship* bank account to draw on later when you need it. To criti-cize the sellers' property at this time won't loosen them up to accept a lower price, and it may turn them against you. Sure, the property needs work, but wait until later in the negotiations to detail the repairs and fix-up the house requires. On your first visit to the property, converse, observe, and learn.

A Win-Win Example

> **Before you negotiate in earnest, establish a relationship bank.**

In one of my earliest face-to-face negotiations, I learned the value of win-win. The sellers and I were sitting at their dining room table drafting a contract point by point. The first point was price. Although the sellers had their house priced fairly, I offered $5,000 less. The sellers rejected. I said, "Well, let's put that issue on hold and see if we can agree on some of the other points." In abbreviated form, I was able to get the sellers to agree to:

- A lease-purchase plan with closing 15 months after I took possession of the property
- A cash deposit of just $2,500
- A possession date within six weeks
- Storing all my household furniture in their den for the month prior to my taking possession of the property (I had sold my previous home and was giving quick possession to my buyers, so I was going "homeless" for a month.)
- Including in the sale about $2,000 worth of furniture and appliances

These people were among the easiest sellers I had dealt with. But when we eventually returned to price, they still didn't want to budge. After we talked some more, the husband said, "Look, here's what we paid for the property. At what you're offering us, we would take a $3,000 loss. We want to at least get what we paid."

Here's where negotiation pros differ. Some would say at this point you've got the sellers committed to everything but price. Hang tough and you can still get the price concession you want. The sellers want to close a deal; they won't let you walk away. If they did, they would just have to start over again with someone else—if and when that someone else appears. If they're smart, the sellers won't take that risk.

I don't endorse this hardball approach. If the sellers have been willing to yield on issues important to you, why not let them score a point, too? Once you achieve nearly all you want, why push so hard you might upset the applecart? So, adopting a win-win approach, I increased my offer by $3,000 on the promise the sellers would cut down and remove a dead tree from the backyard. They agreed. We had a deal that pleased us both. (Note: I really wanted this property because its floor plan and window alignments permitted me to create an accessory apartment and several value-enhancing views. The location was superb and the

> **Give and accept will help you sleep at night.**

property was the lowest-priced property in the neighborhood. I knew that even at the sellers' price, I would earn a good profit.)

How to Bargain for a Low Price

Let's return to the beginning of these negotiations. What would have happened early on if we had heavily debated price? Even if I had been able to pull the sellers down to my offer, that "success" probably would have destroyed my chances of getting other things I needed to make the deal work—a hollow victory indeed.

On other occasions, however, I have reversed this approach. When through early inquiries I've learned the sellers have needs stronger than price, I emphasize how I am willing to help them meet those needs (e.g., their preferred moving date, their need to know the transaction is actually going to close). Then, after the sellers understand that they are receiving nearly all of the terms and conditions they want, I justify my request for their concession on price.

Remember, sellers do not demand their price for purely economic reasons. For many, price carries emotional content. A low offer doesn't just hurt their pocketbook. It affronts their pride. They close their minds.

> **Most sellers take lowball offers as personal insults.**

When you debate price alone, more than likely one party "loses" and the other party "wins." When you negotiate (search for) an *agreement,* you and the sellers can both win.

Don't Compromise, Conciliate

The story is told of a mother who hears her two children bickering at the dinner table. Each child wants the only remaining slice of pie. Tiring of this debate, the mother takes the slice, cuts it in two, and gives half to Craig and half to Shawn. "There," she says, "as you get older you've got to realize that you can't have everything you want. You must learn to compromise. Remember this as an important lesson."

| Why split a pie when you can enlarge it? |

This well-intentioned mother thought she was teaching her kids a valuable lesson; in fact, she reinforced a great obstacle to win-win negotiating. She split the difference before she discovered her children's wants and a range of options; this mother mistakenly framed her kids' debate along a single continuum. Compromise simply meant cutting the pie into equal halves.

Look for Ways to Make a Pie Bigger   Had the mother framed the problem differently, more than likely she could have figured out a better solution. What if Shawn really preferred the crust and Craig preferred the filling? What if the children shared a television set and each preferred different programs? What if the children shared after-dinner cleanup responsibilities? What if the children had money from an allowance? What if Shawn didn't really want the pie, but simply liked to torment Craig?

Had the mother recognized a range of wants, trade-offs, and outcomes, she might have produced results more satisfying (or just) for both children. The true art of negotiating doesn't depend on one's readiness to strike a compromise. It depends on seeing beyond a single either/or issue.

Conciliation Sparks Creativity   Earlier, I told how sellers had agreed to let me use one of their rooms to store household furniture. Alternatively, I wanted an earlier date of possession and they wanted a later date. What would have happened had we focused our negotiations exclusively on possession date? I would have said, "I have to be out of my present home on February 1. I need possession on that date."

The sellers might have responded, "We can't get into our new home until March 1. A February 1 possession date is out of the question. We can't possibly give you possession before February 28."

If I'm thinking compromise, I might say, "Let's split the difference. I'll agree on February 15. I'm willing to meet you halfway."

Although meeting the sellers halfway seems to reflect fair play, in many situations it doesn't make sense, or it overlooks another more satisfying outcome. In this case, February 15 was undesirable for both

> **Thoughtful conciliation beats lose-lose compromise.**

of us. So that position never found its way onto the table. Looking at my real problem—what to do with my furniture for a month without incurring the costs of multiple moves into and out of storage—we struck upon the solution of temporarily storing my household goods in a large room they used but didn't really need. We both were satisfied with this outcome.

Compromise Provokes Extremes   People who negotiate to compromise typically open with offers at the extreme. If you believe the sellers will split the difference, it's to your advantage to offer $375,000 for a property that's worth $425,000. Should the sellers agree to meet you halfway, they will sell you the house for $400,000.

But few sellers are that obliging. The tactic of bid low and compromise is too familiar to work effectively. As negotiating expert Herb Cohen likes to emphasize, "A tactic perceived is no tactic at all." You're more likely to succeed if you bake a bigger pie. Expand your knowledge of wants, needs, trade-offs, and possibilities. To paraphrase Emerson, "Foolish compromises are the hobgoblins of little minds."

Learn the Sellers' Reasons and Reference Points

When the sellers say, "This house is worth at least $525,000," learn their reference points. Why do they think $525,00 represents bottom dollar? When the sellers say, "We need at least $525,000," find out why. When the sellers say, "We couldn't afford to carry back financing; we need every net dollar in cash," find out why. No matter what the objection to your proposal, never accept it as the last word. Find the underlying reasons and the foundation that the sellers are building to support their decision (or their counterproposal).

> **Find out where the sellers are coming from.**

Fast-talking sales agents deal with objections like a steamroller. They charge forward and flatten the prospect's reluctance without bothering to slow down, let alone stop, look, and listen. In contrast, never "overcome objections" by the methods taught in those high-pressure sales training classes. Correct, alleviate, or eliminate the sellers' misperceptions through better understanding.

If it turns out that the sellers' facts or perceptions do make sense, solve their problem—do not steamroll their objections. A confused mind says no. To evoke a *yes*, assuage the sellers' real concerns.

Use an Agent as an Intermediary, but Negotiate for Yourself

Writing in a national trade magazine for realtors, sales agent Sal Greer tells of an offer he received on one of his listings. Sal says that after receiving the purchase offer from a *buyer's agent,* this agent told Sal, "This is their [first] offer, but I know my buyers will go up to $150,000."

"Of course," Sal adds, "I told my sellers that information, and we were pleased with the outcome of the transaction."

The lesson here is clear. Never let your agent negotiate for you. Conceal agent information you do not want the other side to learn. Withhold the idea that you will pay a price higher than your first offer. Use your agent as a fact finder and intermediary. Guard your emotions, confidences, and intentions.

First-time investors rely too heavily on their agents to come up with the terms of their offer and carry out their negotiations. Such investors ask their agents, "What price do you think I should offer? What's the most you think I should pay? Will the sellers concede points or agree to carryback financing?" The buyers then follow whatever the agent recommends.

> **Never abandon control of negotiations to your agent (or your attorney).**

These buyers abdicate their responsibilities. If you follow their example and shift decision making to your agent, you run the following risks.

You May Be Working with a Subagent   Remember, you may be working with the sellers' subagent. As a subagent, a Realtor's legal duty is to the seller. In favoring the sellers' interests, the agent may persuade you to boost the price or terms of your offer. Or the agent may disclose your confidences to the sellers.

As a practical matter, many subagents don't strictly follow the letter of the law. Even though technically they represent the sellers, in their heart they may feel more loyalty to a buyer. I know subagents who work hard for their investors—even to the detriment of sellers.

Nevertheless, since you don't know how your agent will use the information you share, limit your disclosures. Likewise, when it comes to offering price and terms, rely on your agent for facts about the sellers, selling prices of comp houses, neighborhood statistics, and market conditions. Listen to the agent's price recommendations and accept the benefits of his or her knowledge and experience. But don't delegate decision making. You may give up more than you need to.

> **Buyers' agents, too, face conflicts of interest.**

Be Cautious of Buyers' Agents Increasingly, brokerage firms promote buyers' agents. Since sellers are represented by their own agents, buyers need someone to look out for their interests. Marilyn Wilson, a Bellingham, Washington, real estate broker, says, "Buyers should think of their agents as attorneys. Would you want to have one attorney representing both parties in a divorce settlement?"

Superficially, the idea sounds reasonable. Yet even if you choose to employ a buyers' agent, guard your disclosures and negotiating strategy. Like the buyers' agent Sal Greer referred to earlier, even *your* agent may disclose confidences—either intentionally or unintentionally.

We're all subject to subtle influences. A buyers' agent may talk you into offering a higher price because it will make his or her job easier. Under which scenario do you think an agent will work hardest for you: when the agent knows you offered $885,000 but you've said you're willing to go to $910,000, or when you offer $885,000 and say, "If they don't accept this offer, there's four or five other properties I'd like to look at"?

Watch What You Say Regardless of whether you work with a sellers' subagent, a buyers' agent, a dual agent, or a facilitator, watch what you say. Don't tell your agent everything and then turn the negotiations over to her. In fact, it doesn't matter whether we're talking about lawyers, insurance agents, financial planners, real estate agents, or other professional relationships, conflict of interest lurks in the background. Walk a fine line. Release enough information to achieve the results you want, but not so much that you invite your advisor to sacrifice your interests to the interests of someone else (including herself).

The Deal's Not Over till It's Over

"I chose to work with a buyers' agent," recalls Barry Tausch. "I felt a buyers' agent would push harder to get me the best deal possible. As it turned out, I pushed too hard.

All types of agents sometimes compromise their principals (and principles).

"I knew the sellers were getting a divorce. The wife had moved out of the house and in with her boss. Without income from the wife's paycheck, the husband faced tough times. He couldn't handle the household expenses on his own. Although they had a lot of equity in the house, the husband was hurting for cash. He needed a fast sale. By using this information to my advantage, I got the sellers to come down at least $20,000 to $25,000 below market. Bad deal for them. Good deal for me.

"The only thing I had to agree to was a 30-day close. I didn't think this would be a problem because I already had been preapproved. But it was. There was one foul-up after another.

"In the meantime, the sellers got a backup offer for $7,500 more than my price. The husband resented me for 'stealing' his house; he wouldn't cut any slack. When I missed the loan commitment date, he demanded payment. When I couldn't deliver, he pulled the contract and sold to the backup buyers."

Beware of pushing too far, too hard.

Leave Something on the Table Negotiating expert Bob Woolf says, "There isn't any contract I have negotiated where I didn't feel I could have gone for more money or an additional benefit. Why leave money on the table? Because skilled negotiators know the deal's not over till it's over. If you push too hard, you antagonize the other party." Even if they've signed a contract, they start thinking of all the ways they can get out of it. If you stumble on the way to closing, they won't help you up. They'll just kick dirt in your face.

In the purchase of real estate—where emotions run strong—leave something on the table. The purchase agreement forms stage one of your negotiations. Later, you might hit problems with property inspections, appraisal, financing, possession date, closing date, surveys, zoning, building permits, or other issues. Without goodwill, trust, and cooperation, setbacks on the way to closing can throw your agreement into contentious dispute.

Let Profit Guide Your Negotiations   As a potential investor in fixers and renovations, you can become (1) a cutthroat shark (hardballer), (2) an accommodator, or (3) a win-win conciliator.

The Shark   As a shark, you reach across the table and pull as many of the sellers' chips as possible into your pile. In most cases, that tactic will get you kicked out of the game. "That's okay," some investors reply, "I can find another table at which to play. Sooner or later, I'll dupe the other side into losing a sucker bet."

It's true. You can win big at the expense of someone else. How often? As the gurus who promote such tactics admit, "Maybe 1 out of 50 or 1 out of 100 times. You must persist. It's a numbers game." This approach works best for those people who can spend many hours looking at deals. For most investors, the big payoffs won't compensate for the heavy commitment of time, effort, and rejections.

The Accommodator   Accommodators never offend. They never want to lose a deal. They fear rejection. They see the promise but fail to tally the risks. Accommodators buy a lot of properties, but they fail to make any serious money. Their enthusiasm for the deal causes them to give in too easily to the sellers' requests. As a result they make commitments they cannot honor. They agree to pay prices that rarely yield high profits.

> **Never reject without first exploring a range of possibilities.**

The Win-Win Conciliator   Here's the style where real estate investors make the most money. As a conciliator, you won't quickly say yes, and you won't quickly say no. You'll learn all you can about the market, the sellers, and the property. Most importantly, know yourself: What are your resources? What are your talents? What are the sources and amounts of your funding? What are your profit goals?

With knowledge of the market, the sellers, the property, and yourself in view, you work cooperatively with the sellers to shape your deal points. Some will be in your pile, some in the sellers' pile. To strike the best win-win deals, you negotiate only with those sellers whose most crucial wants and needs fit together with yours like the pieces of a jigsaw puzzle. The sellers need what you can give. You need what the sellers can give. The skilled conciliator brings all the pieces together to form a picture of profits.

CHAPTER 11

Easy Money for Owner-Occupants

No matter what your finances or credit look like, this chapter shows you how to raise the money to buy, renovate, and flip properties. Your possibilities multiply when you bring cash and credit into the deal. But neither flipping nor buy-and-hold require these advantages.

Owner-Occupied Financing

> **New loan programs make buying easier.**

During the past five years, mortgage lenders have created dozens of little- or nothing-down payment mortgages for homebuyers. Although some of these loan programs restrict financing to buyers who have not owned a home for a period of at least three years, others are open to anyone with passable credit and a steady source of income.

Though the recent so-called subprime crisis has taken some of the more foolish loan programs off the menu, you still can choose from a good selection of little- or nothing-down financing techniques.

Passable Credit

What is "passable credit"? Typically, it is a FICO score of 620 (possibly lower). (To learn your FICO scores, go to www.myfico.com.) Passable credit even includes people with previous foreclosures and bankruptcies—as long as these borrowers can reasonably explain their lapses and have reestablished credit for a period of at least one and preferably two years.

Attention Current Homeowners

> **Owner-occupants receive the lowest interest and easiest terms.**

If you already own a home and are short of cash, consider this strategy: Locate a property that offers strong renovation potential. Find a tenant for your current home. Apply for a low-down-payment, owner-occupied mortgage. Move into your fixer (obviously, I'm not talking about a house that's an unlivable junker) and work on getting the property renovated during your spare time. If you can do it, this tactic offers the following advantages—depending on the specific details of your renovation plan and the type of financing you use:

◆ Low or no down payment
◆ Easier qualifying for the mortgage loan
◆ No extra carrying costs during the renovation period
◆ Assumable financing for your buyer when you sell the property
◆ Lower cost of interest than you would pay with straight investor financing
◆ Possible tax-free capital gain on sale (if you stay in the property for two years, or if you move for "unforeseen circumstances" prior to a two-year residency)

If you want to build wealth fast, get into owner-occupied fixers. No technique offers as many advantages with so little risk. Whether you rent or own, consider this profit-generating strategy.

FHA 203(k): The Homebuyer's Best Choice for Financing

Like most other renters, Quentlin Henderson of Orlando, Florida, hoped to own his own home someday. Yet, with little savings, Quentlin thought he wouldn't realize his hopes for at least three to four years. He never dreamed that within six months he would actually own a completely renovated, three-bedroom, two-bath home of 2,288 square feet—more than two and a half times as large as his previous 900-square-foot apartment.

> **Turn a fixer into fast profits with FHA 203(k).**

How did Quentlin manage this feat? He discovered the little-known but increasingly available FHA 203(k) mortgage loan program. FHA 203(k) allows any homebuyer to acquire and improve a rundown property with a low- or no-down-payment loan. "The house needed a new roof, new paint, new carpeting; and a bad pet odor needed to be removed," says Quentlin. "There is no way I could have paid for the house plus the repairs at the same time. And there was no way I could have otherwise afforded a house this size."

Locate an FHA 203(k) Specialist   To use a 203(k) plan, your first step is to locate a realtor or mortgage loan advisor who understands the current FHA 203(k) purchase and improvement process. In the past, FHA often stuck borrowers in red tape for months without end. But now, with recent FHA streamlining and special computer software, Robert Arrowwood of California Financial Corporation reports that up-to-date, direct endorsement (DE) firms like his can close 203(k) loans in four to six weeks instead of four to six months.

Search for Good Value   Once you've located 203(k) advisors who know what they're doing, your next step is to search for a property that offers good value for the money. In Quentlin Henderson's case, his Realtor found him a bargain-priced, six-year-old house that was in a sorry state because its former owners had abandoned it as a result of foreclosure. "The good news for people who buy such houses," says Bob Osterman of HUD/FHA's Orlando, Florida, office, "is that prices are generally so low that after repairs are made, the home's new value often produces instant equity."

Not surprisingly, the term *instant equity* was also used by John Evianiak, a 203(k) buyer in Baltimore. "Not only can you buy a house and fix it the way you like," John says, "but you can buy a house for much below its market value, put some money into it, and create instant equity. There were a lot of other houses we checked out. But we were going by the profit margin."

> **Only use a 203(k)
> loan specialist.**

Inspect, Design, and Appraise   Locate a property that you can buy and renovate profitably. With purchase agreement in hand, the property is then inspected, a formal plan of repair and renovation is designed, and the property is appraised according to its value after your improvements have been completed. The amount of your loan is based upon your purchase price plus your rehab expenses up to nearly 100 percent of the property's renovated value.

> **You can finance
> almost any type
> of improvements.**

Eligible Properties and Improvements   As long as you pay more than $5,000 in fix-up expenses, you can use a 203(k) mortgage to acquire and improve nearly any one- to four-unit property. Using 203(k) money, you can convert a single-family house into a two-, three-, or four-unit property. Or you can convert a multifamily property into a duplex or single-family home. As long as you create value, you can rightsize the property in either direction. You may even be able to borrow more than the property will be worth after you complete your improvements. In that case, you can give your buyer a zero-down purchase and loan assumption.

In terms of specific repairs and renovations, the 203(k) mortgage permits a long list of possibilities. Stay away from luxuries (e.g., saunas and hot tubs—although you can spend to repair such items if they're already installed); otherwise, you can do about anything you want. Here are some examples:

- Install skylights, fireplaces, energy-efficient items, or new appliances (stove, refrigerator, washer, dryer, trash compactor, dishwasher).
- Finish off an attic or basement.
- Eliminate pollution or safety hazards (e.g., lead paint, mold, asbestos, underground storage tanks).
- Add living units such as an accessory apartment or two.
- Add baths, bedrooms, a den, or a second story.
- Recondition or replace plumbing, roof, or HVAC systems.
- Improve aesthetic appeal (paint, carpet, tile, exterior siding).
- Install or replace a well or septic system.
- Landscape and fence the yard.

"One of the great features of this program is that it doesn't restrict the niceties," says Michael Noel of Pinnacle Financial. "If you want to install upgraded kitchen cabinets, you can do that. If you want to add crown moldings, you can do it. You can't borrow the money to install a swimming pool, but you can use the money—up to $1,500—to fix up an existing swimming pool."

> **Fannie and Freddie offer 203(k) look-alike programs.**

FHA 203(k) Look-Alike Programs   Fannie Mae, Freddie Mac, various portfolio lenders, and some city redevelopment agencies offer mortgages that combine property acquisition costs and renovation expenses into one loan. Also, some hard money lenders (see discussion on page 229) permit you to wrap purchase price and repairs in the same loan. Absent this all-in-one feature, you need to supplement your purchase money mortgage with additional funding for renovations.

Usually, that's not a problem. FHA and other lenders provide property improvement loans. But applying for and taking out two loans can stick you with more red tape and higher loan costs. Nevertheless, because non-owner-occupant investors can't use FHA 203(k), many, and possibly most, investor rehab projects do involve multiple sources of funding.

Owner-Occupied Purchase Loans

Either an owner-occupant or investor with passable credit can easily obtain a mortgage with 20 to 30 percent down (and sometimes as low as 10 percent down). With 20 percent down (or more), you can borrow from just about any mortgage lender. If as an owner-occupant you either can't (or don't want to) put more than 5 percent down, you might choose from any of the following mortgage loans.

FHA Acquisition Mortgages   In addition to the FHA 203(k) rehab loan, HUD/FHA authorizes easy-qualify, low-down-payment (3 to 5 percent) mortgages to buy condominiums, manufactured homes, single-family houses, duplexes, triplexes, and quads (as long as you live in one of the units). FHA not only underwrites 15- and 30-year fixed-rate loans, it offers adjustable-rate (ARMs), graduated payment (GPMs), and property improvement loans.

> **Any borrower with passable credit can use FHA loans.**

Not Limited to Low Income   Contrary to what many authors write, FHA does not limit its loans to low-income families, first-time homebuyers, or low-priced properties. Anyone who legally resides in the United States can seek an FHA loan regardless of how many properties they've previously owned or the amount of their income. As to mortgage limits, FHA offers the following:

FHA Mortgage Limits* (2008)

	Basic Limits	Higher-Cost Areas
Single family	$200,160	$362,790
Duplex	256,248	464,449
Triplex	309,744	561,411
Quad	384,936	697,696

*Congress has proposed much higher limits. Verify current law.

> **FHA runs the largest loan program in the country.**

To learn the exact FHA mortgage limits that apply in your area, look under mortgages in the Yellow Pages of your telephone directory. Then find the display ad of a lender who specializes in FHA loans. These lenders are called *direct endorsement (DE) underwriters*. DE lenders can directly approve your FHA loan without submitting any paperwork to FHA. You can also learn about FHA (and HUD homes, too) at www.hud.gov.

Advantages of FHA   Each year, hundreds of thousands of homebuyers choose some type of FHA loan. FHA leads the low-down-payment category because it offers these six advantages:

1. You can roll many of your closing expenses and mortgage insurance premiums into your loan. This cuts the out-of-pocket cash you'll need at closing.
2. You may choose from either fixed-rate or adjustable-rate FHA plans. (As an aside, note that FHA ARMs give you lower annual and lifetime caps than most non-FHA ARM programs.)
3. FHA authorizes banks and other lenders to use higher qualifying ratios and easier underwriting guidelines. If your credit and income meet "passable" standards, FHA will do all it can to approve your loan. FHA wants to approve more loans for homebuyers.
4. If interest rates drop (and as long as you have a clean mortgage payment record for the past 12 months), you can "streamline"

refinance your FHA loan at lower interest rates without a new appraisal and without having to requalify.

5. If you can persuade parents or other close relatives to "gift" you the down payment, you won't need to come up with any down payment cash from your own pocket.

6. Unlike most nongovernment, fixed–rate loans, FHA mortgages are assumable. The person who buys your property won't necessarily have to apply for a new mortgage. When mortgage interest rates are high, an assumable mortgage gives your property a great selling advantage. As a fix-and-flip homebuyer/investor, you should find the assumability feature especially attractive.

FHA Drawbacks   Besides somewhat limited loan amounts, FHA mortgages display several other drawbacks. For one, you must buy FHA mortgage insurance (MIP) to protect the lender should you fail to make your mortgage payments. Currently, mortgage insurance costs around 1.5 percent of the amount you borrow (e.g., $1,500 per $100,000 of mortgage—if you lack cash, add this premium into your mortgage loan balance). Plus, your loan rate will increase by one-half percent to cover additional mortgage insurance premiums that FHA requires with your monthly mortgage payments.

> **FHA has helped more first-time buyers than any other loan program.**

The Verdict on FHA   Misinformation and ignorance unjustly surrounds the FHA program. In reality, when you match the benefits of FHA loans to their costs, FHA comes out a winner.

If you can start your fix-up career as an owner-occupant, compare FHA (especially 203(k)) to other loans. Unless you find a seller who offers easy OWC financing, FHA often proves to be your best choice.

Fannie/Freddie Low-Down Loans   Fannie Mae and Freddie Mac do not directly loan mortgage money to homebuyers (owner-occupants) or investors (non-owner-occupants). However, these huge players in the mortgage market do set the underwriting standards for thousands of mortgage lenders throughout the country. And, in recent years, both of these companies have substantially increased their 5 percent, 3 percent, and in some cases, even zero-down homebuyer loans. (Fannie and Freddie approve loans for investors with 15 to 20 percent down.)

Typically, Fannie/Freddie loan products charge less for mortgage insurance than FHA. But they apply stricter credit standards. Neither Fannie nor Freddie (explicitly) permits buyers to assume their fixed-rate loans (as do FHA and VA). Currently, Fannie/Freddie loans apply the following loan limits:

Fannie/Freddie Mortgage Limits (2008)*

Single family	$417,000
Duplex	533,850
Triplex	645,300
Quad	801,950

*Congress has proposed much higher limits. In Alaska, Hawaii, Guam, and the U.S. Virgin Islands, Fannie/Freddie limits are increased by 50 percent.

Fannie Mae's 203(k) look-alike rehab program is called UFIXIT. Fannie/Freddie loans are called *conventional, conforming mortgages.* Most major mortgage lenders offer loan products designed by either Fannie or Freddie.

> **VA offers veterans a great mortgage program, yet most veterans don't use it.**

Department of Veterans Affairs The VA mortgage is one of the best benefits offered to those who have worn our country's uniform. Here are several of the benefits the VA mortgage offers:

◆ No down payment. With a VA loan you can finance up to $417,000 without putting any money down. If you want to buy a higher-priced home, you need only come up with 25 percent of the amount over $417,000. For instance, if the home you want to buy is priced at $517,000, you'll need a down payment of $25,000 (.25 X $100,000)—or just 4.8 percent of the purchase price.

◆ Similar to FHA, VA loans offer liberal qualifying guidelines. Many (but not all) VA lenders will forgive properly explained credit blemishes. The VA loan also permits higher qualifying ratios. I've seen veterans with good compensating factors close loans with a .48 total debt ratio.

◆ Often new homebuilders and cooperative sellers will pay all of the veteran's settlement expenses. In fact, new homebuilders sometimes advertise that veterans can buy homes in their developments for just one dollar total move-in costs.

◆ Like FHA, a buyer may assume your VA mortgage when you sell the property. Like FHA, if interest rates fall, you can streamline a no-appraisal, no-qualifying refinance.

◆ Unlike FHA, when you use a VA loan, you do not buy mortgage insurance. You will, however, pay a one-time "funding fee" ranging between 1 and 2.25 percent of the amount you borrow. If you don't pay this fee in cash at closing, you can add it to your mortgage loan.

> **Always work with a VA lending specialist.**

As with many types of mortgages, VA loans require piles of paperwork and compliance with various guidelines that look into job history, property condition, home value (called a CRV), and seller prepaids. So, work with a mortgage loan advisor who is skilled in getting VA loans approved. "The devil is in the details," says loan consultant Abe Padoka. Make sure you work with professionals who know the ins and outs of the VA (or FHA) loan approval process.

Community Loan Programs   When nationally syndicated ("Nation's Housing") columnist Kenneth Harney wrote, "Mortgage lenders devise more ways to say yes," he referred to community loan products. "If you don't own a home because you assume that your income, cash savings, or job history rule you out, think again," Harney advises. "Banks, thrifts, and other mortgage lenders are actually rewriting their rulebooks to get you into home ownership."

> **Community loan programs may help get a neighborhood revitalized.**

Look, You'll Find Them To locate community loan programs in your area, call banks, savings institutions, and mortgage companies. Speak to a loan officer or assistant vice-president who knows that lender's community lending or community reinvestment (CRA) loan programs. Some lenders refer to these (or similar) easier-qualifying loans as "first-time buyer" programs. Because community lending has grown quickly, your efforts to locate the right program may take your fingers for a walk through the Yellow Pages. But your reward will make the trip worthwhile.

Low-Down, Easier Qualifying Although it's unusual to find a no-down-payment community lending program, you will turn up a relaxed qualifying, 3- to 5-percent-down home-finance plan. Ask Realtors, loan officers, and friends who have recently bought homes. Closely read the mortgage loan ads in your local newspapers. Ask a Realtor to look through the monthly (or quarterly) magazine published by the state's association of Realtors. Often, these publications include articles and ads that describe the recently developed, easier-qualifying home-finance plans.

Down Payment Assistance From Oakland, California, to Atlanta, Georgia, from Boston to Miami, from Chicago to Houston, city and county governments and not-for-profit housing organizations have been providing down payment assistance to persons who have not owned a home during the past three years. Typically, these grants range from $1,500 to $5,000, but I've seen them go as high as $15,000. See, for example, the front-page *Wall Street Journal* article, "Buyers Get Free Down Payments on Homes" (December 10, 2002).

> **Local governments give buyers down payment money.**

To learn the types of down payment assistance that are offered in your area, telephone your city or county department of housing, finance, or community development. Often these programs fit right in with your efforts to buy and renovate fixers because they may be targeted toward neighborhoods to prime them for revitalization. The same government and not-for-profit agencies may also provide low-cost money to cover rehab and renovation expenses.

Owner-Occupied Assumptions

> **Real estate gurus popularized the non-quals.**

Up until the early 1980s, owners who sold their properties could transfer their mortgages to their buyers. In many cases, to take advantage of this mortgage assumption, the buyers weren't even required to go through any type of qualifying process. These loans (chiefly underwritten by FHA and VA) were called *nonqualifying assumables.*

When the nothing-down gurus of the 1970s and 1980s told their readers, "No cash, no credit, no problem," these gurus were urging their readers to buy properties from sellers who offered non-qual assumable mortgages. "Find motivated sellers," the gurus advised. "Then talk them into a deal where you simply step in and pick up their mortgage payments. Equity? No problem. Give the sellers a second mortgage, or maybe trade them your RV."

> **Nonqualifying assumables have virtually disappeared.**

> **Many types of *qualifying* assumptions are readily available.**

The End of an Era   Alas, those simpler days are gone. By 1982, Congress, the courts, and mortgage contracts had terminated the *right* of assumption for conventional, conforming, fixed-rate mortgages. Then in the late 1980s, both FHA and VA removed their contract clauses that permitted nonqualifying assumptions from all future mortgage originations.

Today, as a practical matter, you won't find any remaining non-quals that could work to your advantage.

What Assumption Possibilities Can You Pursue?   Even though the non-quals have disappeared, owner-occupants with *qualifying* passable credit may pursue several other types of mortgage assumptions:

1. *All outstanding FHA mortgages.* As an owner-occupant with passable credit, you can assume any fixed-rate or adjustable-rate mortgage.
2. *All outstanding VA mortgages.* With passable credit, you can assume any outstanding VA mortgage.
3. *Many outstanding conventional, adjustable-rate mortgages.* With good credit (FICO of 620 to 680 or above), you can assume a Fannie/Freddie ARM and ARMs written by portfolio lenders (those lenders who set their own underwriting standards apart from Fannie, Freddie, FHA, or VA).
4. *Nearly all outstanding conventional fixed-rate mortgages with lender approvals.* Unlike assumption possibilities 1 through 3 above, conventional fixed-rate loans may *not* be assumed as a matter of right—regardless of the creditworthiness of the buyer. However, a lender—at its discretion—may permit sellers to transfer their mortgage to the buyer of their property.

Implications for Owner-Occupant Renovators Depending on the lender and the amount you borrow, a newly originated mortgage can typically cost you anywhere from $3,000 to $10,000 in settlement expenses. When you assume a mortgage, your settlement costs will probably run less than $1,000. If you plan to fix and flip a property, mortgage origination costs can bite a large chunk out of your profits, whereas if you buy a property and assume the seller's existing loan, you save settlement dollars for yourself.

Always learn the particulars of a seller's existing financing. What balance remains outstanding on the original loan? How might a buyer assume the loan? At what interest rate? Pursue this line of inquiry when you negotiate with owners who are behind in their mortgage payments. Even lenders who do not usually allow assumptions may be persuaded to do so on favorable terms. (For a more extensive discussion of financing, see Gary W. Eldred, *106 Mortgage Secrets All Borrowers Must Learn— But Lenders Don't Tell* [2nd ed., Wiley, 2008].)

CHAPTER 12

Money for Anyone

We now leave the land of mortgages that are available to owner-occupants and enter a world of property financing where everyone can play.

"Subject to" versus Mortgage Assumptions

Say you would like to buy a property and take advantage of its current financing. Unfortunately, either the loan does not permit an assumption or for one reason or another (credit problems, uncertain or unprovable income, non-owner-occupant, etc.), the lender won't qualify you to take over the existing loan. Is there another way to do the deal and keep the financing intact? Yes—it's called a *subject-to purchase*.

With today's mortgage assumptions, a lender releases the sellers from personal liability for their mortgage payments and allows you to take over their responsibilities. When you buy a property *subject to* the mortgage(s), you pay the sellers their equity (if any) in cash or with a note. The sellers deed you their property. No one tells the lender what's going on. You make the monthly payments for principal, interest, property taxes, and insurance. The lender still holds its mortgage lien against the property as collateral, but you're now the owner.

> **"Subject to" provides great short-term financing for fix and flip.**

Is This Technique Legal?

Contrary to what some people believe, the subject-to technique is neither illegal, immoral, or fattening. However, it *may* trigger the so-called *due-on-sale clause*, which is paragraph number 18 in the Fannie/Freddie fixed-rate mortgage contract. In part, the due-on-sale clause reads as follows:

> If all or any part of the [mortgaged] property or an interest therein is sold or transferred by the Borrower *without Lender's prior written consent . . . Lender may, at Lender's option, declare* all sums secured by this Mortgage to be immediately *due and payable.*

"Subject to" is perfectly legal.

Notice that nothing in this paragraph prevents owners from selling their properties to their buyers without paying off their mortgage. This clause merely gives lenders the right to call the mortgage due and payable if such a transfer occurs without "Lender's prior written consent." If and when the lender learns about the transfer of ownership of the mortgaged property, it may demand payment of the outstanding mortgage balance within 30 days. If you or the sellers don't pay the full amount due, the lender could file a foreclosure lawsuit.

Should You Worry?

Lenders might accelerate long-term subject-to's when interest rates go up.

Note the key words: *if, when,* and *may.* The lender can demand full payment only *if* and *when* it finds out about the title change to the property. Given the bureaucratic communication channels that exist within the loan servicing function of most mortgage lenders, the sellers would not likely receive a demand letter for at least three to six months after you bought the property. Then the foreclosure process could drag on (or be purposely strung out) for another 3 to 12 months (such as when you file a plausible defense or counterclaim).

So, in the event the lender learns of what you and the sellers have pulled off, you enjoy at least a six-month window of opportunity to renovate and sell (or refinance) the property. For the majority of fix and flips, six months provide plenty of time to get in and out of the deal.

But this worst-case scenario presumes the lender will issue a demand letter. In practice, lenders do not push a performing mortgage into foreclosure. To do so could transform a paying asset into a losing asset. Because such a policy seldom makes sense, few lenders pursue it. Pay the mortgage, taxes, and insurance on time and, as most lender operating procedures now stand, you need not lose sleep worrying about a due-on-sale clause.

Short Term, Not Long Term

"No worries" refers to a short-term fix-and-flip or a short-term fix-and-refinance strategy. Over the long term, you could face a mortgage call risk if market interest rates shoot up. In that case, lenders *might* aggressively enforce the due-on-sale clause.

Conventional lenders eliminated the *right* of assumption clause because, during the late 1970s and early 1980s, high inflation and higher costs of deposits forced many savings and loans (S&Ls) into insolvency. S&Ls were paying depositors 8 to 12 percent interest on their savings and certificates of deposit, yet those old assumable mortgages that were still on the lenders' books were bringing in just 5 to 8 percent. To survive, lenders must bring in more from mortgage interest earnings than they pay in interest costs to their depositors. In times of rapidly rising interest rates, lenders want their outstanding low-interest loans paid off as soon as possible.

Risks to Sellers

With a mortgage assumption, the lender qualifies buyers of the property. When buyers meet the approval standards, the lender issues a novation or "release of liability" to the sellers. The sellers now get off the hook. What-ever happens to that mortgage in the future does not concern them.

Not so with subject-to deeds. In those cases, the sellers' credit and finances remain at risk for as long as the mortgage remains outstanding. If the buyers pay the mortgage late, the lender reports the sellers to the credit bureaus. If the property goes into foreclosure, the lender will chase down the sellers for any money (deficiency) judgment the court awards. A subject-to agreement places the sellers at risk.

Your Borrowing Strategy

When you apply for property financing, use solid evidence to persuade the lender that you will pay the money back as agreed. This same principle stands true for seller-assisted financing. To make your case, rely on the following criteria:

- ◆ *Credit.* If you've built a strong credit record, prove it with your FICO scores, a credit report, or a letter from your landlord (if you're currently renting).
- ◆ *Income.* Pull out your W-2s, 1099s, or income tax returns. Show your financial capacity to make the payments.
- ◆ *Property.* Emphasize your plans to create value for the property (but only to the extent that you don't weaken your negotiating position on price).
- ◆ *Commitment.* Impress the sellers with your ambition and commitment to succeed. Many older property owners like to help younger people get started. (This tactic certainly worked for me when I started out and relied on seller-assisted financing.)
- ◆ *Character.* No one wants to do business with someone they do not trust. Throughout your rapport building and negotiation with the sellers, present yourself (both directly and indirectly) as a person of integrity. If you've experienced credit problems, explain them in terms of circumstances beyond your control— not financial irresponsibility.

> **Many sellers need persuading.**

At first, most property owners respond coolly to subject-to offers to purchase. But, when you put forth convincing assurances and protections, you often can persuade flexible or motivated sellers to accept such an agreement. (I have used subject-to agreements to buy and sell a number of properties.)

Seller-Assisted Financing

If you can't negotiate a mortgage assumption or subject-to purchase, fund your purchase by drawing on seller-assisted financing.

When the late nationally syndicated real estate attorney and investor, Robert Bruss, was asked, "Where's the best place to get a mortgage—at a bank, savings and loan, or credit union?," Bob Bruss answered, "None of these is the best. The best source of financing for your property is the seller." If you can persuade the sellers to help with your financing, you can often get easier qualifying and lower costs. Along this same line, here's what Realtor Robert Deimel says about seller financing: "In today's complex marketplace," Robert observes, "sellers and buyers don't always see the opportunity. That's why innovative salespeople are often necessary to open their eyes. The key to making more transactions happen is to understand why and when sellers may want to offer the carrot of seller financing." What are the benefits of seller-assisted financing? Here are several:

> **Seller financing helps close sales that would otherwise fall through.**

- *Easier qualifying.* Although lenders have eased up on their qualifying criteria (relative to a decade ago), they're still stricter than many sellers.
- *Flexibility.* Price, interest rate, monthly payments, and other terms are set by mutual agreement. You and the sellers can schedule repayment in any way that works for both of you.

◆ *Lower closing costs.* Sellers seldom require points, origination fees, and loan application costs. Unlike lenders, sellers don't have to pay office overhead.

◆ *Less paperwork.* Although sellers may ask for credit scores, they won't require a stack of forms, documents, and verifications. (To enhance credibility, though, you may still want to provide such supporting confirmations.)

◆ *Quicker sale.* Seller financing can help owners sell more quickly. For properties that require extensive repairs or renovations, seller financing can make the difference between a sale and no sale.

◆ *Higher returns.* Seller financing often earns sellers a higher interest rate than they could gain from a savings account or certificate of deposit.

◆ *Income tax savings.* Sellers who accept installment payments (rather than a lump sum at closing) pay less tax on their sales proceeds.

◆ *Higher selling price.* Seller financing can help owners sell near the top of their property's price range. (From your perspective, don't overpay. But within reason, you might agree to trade off a somewhat higher price for favorable terms.)

The seller-assisted financing that you might structure is as varied as your and the seller's imagination. In fact, many owners accept seller-assisted financing even when they don't advertise their willingness. Robert Bruss says, "I've bought many houses with seller financing. But I can't recall a single one that was advertised 'seller financing.' Until they saw my offer, none of the sellers had informed their agent that they would help finance the sale."

Likewise, my experiences with OWC match those of Bruss. Ask, persuade, and you might receive.

First Mortgage or Deed of Trust

In some OWC sales, the sellers will convey the title of their property to you and then record a mortgage (or in some states, a deed of trust)

> **Sellers can offer a mortgage just like a bank.**

in the public records. This mortgage (trust deed) serves as a lien against the property. When you buy a property with a seller first mortgage (trust deed), your agreement with the seller establishes rights and responsibilities like those of a bank-financed purchase.

Buy on the Installment Plan

In the classic silent film series, *The Perils of Pauline,* Oil Can Harry repeatedly warned Pauline, "If you don't give me the deed to your ranch, I'm going to tie you to the railroad tracks." Oil Can Harry knew that if Pauline signed over the deed to her ranch, that deed would transfer the property's title to Harry. Although Oil Can Harry's no-money-down approach to property ownership was somewhat unorthodox (not to mention illegal), when you buy real estate, you typically receive a deed at the time of purchase. With the deed comes title and ownership.

> **A contract-for-deed gives you rights to a property but delays transfer of the deed.**

In some sales, though, you do not receive a deed at the time of purchase. Instead, you pay on the installment plan. You give the sellers a down payment and make monthly installments. In return, the sellers turn over possession of the property and promise to deliver a deed to the buyers after they have completed their scheduled payments. Such a purchase agreement is known as an *installment sale, contract-for-deed,* or *land contract.* For buyers and/or properties that do not meet the qualifying criteria of a lender, the land contract serves as a good way to buy property.

> **Land contracts can get almost anyone started in real estate.**

Why Sellers Are Willing   When I turned age 21, I wanted to acquire real estate as quickly as possible, and at the time I was an undergraduate college student. I had little cash, no full-time job, and no formal credit record. My immediate chances for getting a bank to write a mortgage were zero. But this fact didn't deter me. I searched for properties that I could buy on an installment contract. By the time I completed my PhD, I had bought around 30 houses and small apartment buildings. The cash flow from these properties paid my college expenses (as well as for unwise extravagances such as my Cessna and Jaguar XKE).

Land contract sellers achieve all of the benefits listed on pages 220 - 221, but four benefits stand out:

1. *No bank financing available.* A property may not qualify for bank financing. The property might suffer poor maintenance, be located in a declining neighborhood, or be functionally out-of-date (rooming house, apartment units with shared bathrooms, irregular floor plan). Also, many lenders won't write mortgages on condominiums when more than 30 or 40 percent of the units in the complex are occupied by renters instead of owners. In such circumstances, land-contract properties offer opportunities for value-creating entrepreneurs.

2. *High interest on savings.* Sellers who plan to deposit the cash they receive from a sale into certificates of deposit or money market accounts can get a higher return on their money by financing a buyer's purchase of their property. A 7 to 10 percent return from a real estate installment sale certainly beats a 2 to 4 percent return from a certificate of deposit.

3. *Tax savings.* When the seller is an investor, an installment sale of a property produces a smaller income tax bite than does a cash sale.

4. *Repossession.* If a borrower defaults, the installment contract gives sellers a relatively quick and inexpensive right to repossess the property (often without a foreclosure process).

> **Use a contract-for-deed as a short-term finance strategy.**

Follow These Guidelines Because it's simple and low cost, the installment sale works well to help you pull off a highly leveraged (low cash-to-close) purchase. Buy a property you can improve.

Finance it with a low-down-payment installment contract. Create value through fix-up and renovations. Then sell or refinance the property based on its now-higher value. To use this technique profitably, follow these guidelines:

- ◆ *Buy the property, not the financing.* Don't let easy credit draw you into the purchase of an overpriced money trap. When circumstances warrant, pay a price slightly higher than the as-is value. But you would not pay $5,000 for a 1995 Chevy from Easy Ed's "buy here, pay here" used car lot just because Easy Ed will sell it to you with nothing down and low monthly payments. This same principle applies to real estate. Beware of the guru's tactic that says, "You set the price. I'll set the terms." Verify value through your appraisal or other professional opinion.
- ◆ *Beware of hidden defects.* A property that seems underpriced might suffer hidden defects. Obtain experienced estimates for the repairs and renovations you plan. Never "ballpark" or casually figure the costs necessary to bring a property up to the condition you want it. Before you buy, obtain property inspections and reliable cost estimates.
- ◆ *Contract terms are governed by law.* A contract-for-deed places you and the seller in a relationship that is governed not only by the contract language but also by state laws and court decisions. Under an installment sale, your rights and responsibilities differ from those you acquire when you finance a property with a mortgage or trust deed.

> **Don't let the ease of a land contract deter your due diligence.**

Prior to negotiating an installment sale agreement, consult a real estate attorney who is experienced in reviewing these contracts. Develop an understanding of contract law as it applies in your state so that you learn how to structure your deal in a way in which you adequately protect your interests.

However, beware of lawyers who lack knowledge of this contract specialty. Some naysaying risk-averse lawyers warn against buying any property on the installment plan. (Using similar logic, such lawyers would advise against marriage because divorce can be so painful.) This type of lawyer looks at risks without considering benefits and opportunities. Consult a lawyer who understands both. Then negotiate a contract-for-deed that can work for you and the sellers. Over the years, millions of people (especially people who are cash-short and credit-challenged) have successfully bought houses and rental properties on the installment plan.

Lease Option a Property

The lease option combines a lease agreement for a property with an option (the right) to buy that property at a later date. Twenty years ago, real estate columnist and investor Robert Bruss called lease options "the most overlooked and underused" property finance possibility. At that time, most buyers, sellers, and real estate agents remained clueless about this technique.

> **Lease options give you a low-cost, short-term way to control a fixer.**

Times have changed. Awareness has mushroomed. When I travel throughout the United States, I always check through the local real estate classifieds. In most cities, I find real estate agents who routinely handle lease options and other low-down-payment home-finance plans. I have seen lease options promoted by home builders and developers of new condominiums and townhouses. In San Francisco, one ad from Bay Crest Condominiums boldly announced, "If You Can Afford to Rent, You Can Now Afford to Own: Exciting New Lease/ Purchase Option."

With lease options moving into the mainstream, you can easily find lease option sellers. Indeed, when asked, even some "House for Rent" property owners will agree to lease option their rentals. Likewise, some sellers will agree to a lease option (or lease purchase) if you propose it. The lease option gives almost anyone the opportunity to become a homeowner or investor:

- *Easier qualifying.* Qualifying for a lease option may be no more difficult than qualifying for a lease (sometimes easier). Generally, your credit and employment record need meet only minimum standards. Most property owners (sellers or lessors) will not place your financial life under a magnifying glass as would a mortgage lender.

- *Low initial investment.* Your initial investment to get into a lease option agreement can be as little as one month's rent and a security deposit of a similar amount. At the outside, move-in cash rarely exceeds $5,000 to $10,000, although I did see a home lease optioned at a price of $1.5 million that asked for $50,000 up front.

- *Forced savings.* The lease option contract typically forces you to save for the down payment required when you exercise your option to buy. Often, lease options charge above-market rental rates and then credit perhaps 50 percent of your rent toward the down payment. The exact amount is negotiable.

- *Reestablish credit.* A lease option also can help renters buy when they need time to build or reestablish a solid credit record. Judy and Paul Davis wanted to buy a home before prices in their area once again rose above their reach. But the Davises needed time to clear up credit problems created by too much borrowing and Judy's layoff. The lease option could be the possibility that helps the Davises achieve their goal of homeownership.

- *100 percent financing possible.* Lease option a property that can be profitably improved through repairs, renovation, or cosmetics. By increasing the property's value, you may be able to borrow nearly all the money you need to exercise your option to buy. Suppose your lease option purchase price is $175,000, and by the end of one year, your option deposit and rent credits equal $7,500. You now owe the sellers $167,500. Through repairs, fix-up work, and redecorating, you have increased the property's value by $25,000. It's now worth around $200,000. If you have paid your bills on time during the previous year, you can finance the full $167,500 you need to pay off the sellers. As another possibility, sell the property, pay the sellers $167,500,

> **Make sure your lease option gives you enough time to complete your improvements.**

and use the remaining cash from the sale to invest in another property.

The lease option achieves the same objectives as does a land contract installment sale. However, the land contract actually finances the purchase of a property, whereas the lease option puts you on your own to come up with the money to close the deal—before the option to buy expires.

Lease Purchase Agreements versus Lease Purchase Options

Although some people use the terms *lease option* and *lease purchase* interchangeably, technically there's a distinction. With a lease purchase *agreement*, you agree to buy a property. Your lease period merely gives you time to renovate the property, build up cash (or rent credits) for a down payment, or perhaps shape up your financial fitness. With a lease purchase *option* (or more frequently called a *lease option*), you can walk away from the property at the end of your lease period. You would forfeit any option money or rent credits you have paid. But the sellers couldn't require you to go ahead and buy the property if you chose not to.

> **Some sellers prefer a lease purchase (over a lease option) because it seems more solid.**

To buy a property through a lease purchase or lease option agreement, here are six key issues for you and an attorney to decide:

1. *Purchase price.* Verify that the price you offer compares favorably with other similar properties that have recently sold in the neighborhood. When you apply for a mortgage at some future date, the property must appraise high enough to support your desired loan-to-value (LTV) ratio. Some "lease-to-own" sellers grossly overprice their properties and hope to snare a naive buyer.

2. *Move-in cash.* Whether you lease purchase or lease option a property, you negotiate your "move-in" money. The sellers credit this cash toward your purchase price when you eventually buy. If you choose not to buy, the sellers will keep all (or part) of this money.

3. *Lease period.* How much time will you need before you're able to buy? Sellers often want to close relatively quickly—sometimes within 6 to 12 months. However, allow enough breathing room. If you can't renovate the property, sell it, or come up with permanent mortgage financing at the end of your lease period, you may lose your move-in cash. On the other hand, if you can close sooner than the date specified in your agreement, most sellers would gladly accommodate you. (But make sure your agreement gives you that right.)

4. *Rent credits.* Many lease purchase/lease option sellers apply rent credits toward your purchase price. These monthly credits can count as part (or all) of your down payment. But remember, lenders won't count the full amount without question. They count only lease amounts paid in excess of market rent levels. You pay $1,000 a month, the market's at $800, and the lender will allow $200 per month. If you plan to use rent credits as part of your cash to close on permanent financing, make sure your lease agreement fits within the lender's guidelines.

5. *Right to assign.* Include a "right to assign" clause in your agreement. Then if you do not complete your purchase, you can flip (assign for a payment) to someone else, and they can execute at your contract price. That way you won't forfeit all of your rent credits and move-in cash. After you've improved the property, you assign at a premium and profit nicely.

6. *Inspections and title check.* Get the property inspected by a specialist who knows houses. Even when you buy at a steep discount, watch out for the risk of unexpected major repairs. Likewise, pay a title insurer to verify the seller's rights of ownership. Too many lease option/lease purchase buyers omit these precautions and saddle themselves with a poor deal. Discuss this issue with an attorney. Beware of delaying a legal opinion

of title if you give the seller more than a nominal upfront option payment. On occasion, lease option, lease purchase, or contract-for-deed buyers unfortunately learn that the seller has taken their money but can't deliver good title.

Easy Money—Hard Terms

When other types of property financing fail, another possibility exists that I hesitate to recommend, but do so only in the cause of thoroughness. In some limited situations, you can turn to an easy-money lender. Within the real estate industry, such lenders actually work under the label of "private money" or "hard money." I call them "easy-money" lenders because they will loan money to buy, improve, or refinance about any type of property as long as the borrower can fog a mirror.

> **Watch out! "Easy-money" lenders don't play in the same league with FHA/VA or Fannie/Freddie.**

Predatory Lending

In fact, some easy-money lenders loan funds to people who stand little chance of paying it back. Why? Because these lenders *want to foreclose* the property. Such lenders profit from this tactic for three reasons:

1. *Low loan-to-value (L-T-V) ratio.* Easy-money lenders make loans chiefly where the property value exceeds the amount borrowed—i.e., a 60 to 70 percent L-T-V.
2. *Immediate collection.* Unlike reputable mortgage lenders, these easy-money folks don't know the concept of forbearance. Miss a payment and they will sic the lawyers on you as soon as legally possible.
3. *High late fees and penalties.* Not only do these predatory lenders go after the amount owed on the mortgage, they make sure

that the delinquent borrowers pay dearly for their failure to make their payments as scheduled.

State and federal governments have initiated a campaign against predatory lending practices. Two such lenders (Citigroup and Household Lending) have paid a total of $700 million to settle charges of bilking tens of thousands of their mortgage customers.

More recently, Congress has held repeated hearings on predatory abuses in subprime lending—also easy money with hard terms and high costs. Although easy-money lenders make borrowing possible for the credit impaired, these lenders expect to receive a huge (and sometimes illegal or unconscionable) return.

Why Would You Want to Deal with an Easy-Money Lender?

Generally, lenders who specialize in easy money with hard terms appeal to three types of borrowers: (1) the poorly educated who don't really understand the terms and costs of the loan, (2) those who need money so desperately that they'll sign away their future for immediate relief from some financial difficulty, and (3) optimistic property investors who care little about the hard terms of the easy money because they are counting the expected high profits from their venture. Assuming that you're not a type 1 or 2 borrower, let's focus on a type 3 situation.

The Optimistic Entrepreneur

To keep this example simple, assume you find a desperate (aka motivated) property owner who is willing to sell you his $100,000 as-is property for $75,000 if you can come up with the cash within 10 days. You know that with $15,000 and some sweat equity, you could sell the house for at least $135,000. You want to grab this deal before someone else beats you to it. But where can you raise $75,000 on short notice?

You can get it from an easy-money/hard-terms lender. What will this loan cost you? One can't say for sure, because the private mortgage

Hard-terms lenders specialize in fast-cash deals.

industry includes thousands of small players as well as some of the major mortgage lenders like Citigroup (which runs its hard-money and subprime operations through no-name subsidiaries). Each player sets its own costs, terms, and loan-to-value ratios. The structure of the deals varies. Sometimes too much money chases too few borrowers. At other times, too many borrowers chase after too little money.

With these caveats in view, here's how a deal to borrow $75,000 in this situation might look:

	Cash You Pay
Interest @ 15% p.a. (6 months)	$ 5,625
Settlement costs	6,000
Mortgage broker fee @ 5%	3,750
Mortgage payback	75,000
Total cost	90,375
Net cost of funds for 6 months	15,375

	Your Expected Profit
Sales price of renovated property	$135,000
Marketing costs @ 6%	8,100
Cost of funds	15,375
Acquisition cost of property	75,000
Costs of improvements	15,000
Profit (before tax)	21,525

Are these numbers realistic? Yes. Do they reflect a norm? No. Easy-money lenders are idiosyncratic. Each deal is negotiated according to the particulars of the loan, the property, the lender, and the borrower. No Freddie Mac or Fannie Mae sets rules for this mortgage game. Plus, this deal showed a great buy on the property, which is possible but difficult.

Nevertheless, this example does illustrate that, in some cases, you can earn a good profit—even after paying the high costs of a

> **Before you sign up for hard money, take off your rose-colored glasses.**

hard-money lender. Before you enter into such a loan agreement, take off your rose-colored glasses. Sharpen your pencil. Carefully work the numbers. Include a liberal amount for the *oops* factor. If you like the potential profit and can manage the risks, go for it. (From time to time, it even pays to buy experience.)

Where to Find This Easy Money

The classified ad section of many newspapers includes a category entitled "Loans," "Financing," or perhaps "Money to Lend." These advertisers represent easy-money/hard-terms lenders. Look in your telephone book's Yellow Pages under mortgages and mortgage brokers. Look for listings that use language such as "credit problems okay," "nonconforming," "secured," "fast closing," "investor loans," "rehab acquisitions," "we buy mortgages and land contracts," or "no income verification." Figure 12.1 shows a sampling of easy-money ads from the *New York Times* and a local newspaper.

Cash to Close

You can fund your property purchase in many ways. One or more of these techniques will undoubtedly work for you. However, you're not yet in the game because nearly all of these funding techniques will require some cash to close the deal. Where can you get this cash? Here are the most widely used sources:

- ◆ Personal savings and investments
- ◆ Unnecessary assets
- ◆ Home equity loan
- ◆ Partnership ventures

<table>
<tr><td>

PRIVATE LENDER

BRIDGE LOANS, 1 WEEK CLOSING
$500,000 – $300 MILLION
BROKERS WELCOME
201-342-8500

Loans secured by Real Estate,
(even raw land) or any fixed
asset.
No up front fee until agreement
signed
http//www.kennedyfunding.com

COMMERCIAL MORTGAGE
LOANS
LOOK, LIKE & LEND
NO APPRAISAL. 1 WEEK CLOSING
No adv. Fee. LES 212-371-3933

</td><td>

NEED MONEY FAST?

3 day closing. $100K – $10 Million
Real estate secured. No credit
check.
No advance fee. 718-972-9658

COMMERCIAL LOANS

Mixed-use, Multi-Unit Busn.,
Const. No
Fee until agreement. All Type
Credit.
$100K + Low Rates
516-764-5400

A Better Alternative

Good, bad and no credit
Call for 1st & 2nd Mortgages

WE BUY MORTGAGES

Midtown Mortgage Co., Inc.
430-1234
4200 NW 43 St., # A-1

</td></tr>
</table>

Figure 12.1   Newspaper Ads for Easy-Money Lenders.

◆ Second mortgages
◆ Cash advances

Personal Savings

How much cash can you raise from your personal savings and investments?
If your answer comes in at any number less than five figures (not counting decimals!), work through fiscal fitness exercises. (For a philosophy
that leads to sensible spending and wealth building, see *The Millionaire*

Next Door by Thomas Stanley and William Danko [Longstreet Press, 1996].) Financial experts agree that to find money to invest, live *well below* your means.

But even if your bank balance isn't high enough to get you a free checking account, use money from your IRA, 401(k), Keogh, or other tax-deferred accounts (TDAs). The Wall Street mutual funds want to keep that secret from getting out. To tap these funds for your real estate investing, you set up a self-directed account with a third-party administrator. The process follows some complicated rules, but your plan administrator can keep you legal. For more details, go to www.trustetc .com. That's the web site for Equity Trust Company a national firm that shows individuals how to invest their TDA money in real estate of their choosing.

Sell Unnecessary Assets

Can you sell, trade, or downsize any assets such as cars, boats, jet skis, or furniture? What about that no-longer-pursued stamp or coin collection? I recently talked with a would-be investor who lacked cash. "What would you recommend?" she asked. When I queried her about assets, she admitted that she and her husband owned a vacation property at Lake Tahoe with $150,000 of equity.

> **Nearly everyone owns assets that they could sell to raise investment cash.**

"Why don't you sell that property and put the money to more productive use?" I said.

"Well, we've been considering that idea. But we really love our weekend getaways," she said.

"How often do you use the property?" I asked.

"Oh, we don't get over as much as we would like. Maybe four or five times a year."[1]

---

[1]Of course, Lake Tahoe properties themselves have appreciated enormously—but most owners do not generate much rental income from them and the holding costs—interest, property taxes, and upkeep—often eat substantially into the capital gains.

> **Learn to live with less so you can eventually enjoy much more.**

Do you see the problem here? All of us love our possessions. We don't want to give them up. But ask yourself whether those assets are worth the price you pay to own them. I owned a Porsche 911. I loved to drive that car. But when I calculated my out-of-pocket costs of ownership plus the money I could earn by investing the cash that I had tied up in the car, the decision to sell became a no-brainer.

Your decision to sell unnecessary assets becomes even more important when you're shelling out money for monthly payments. Those assets not only imprison your cash, they drag down your credit score and borrowing power. Get rid of unnecessary and extravagant assets. The returns you earn over time will permit you to replace them later many times over. (Or you may find as I have that limiting one's material possessions not only creates a higher quality of life, but also leads to true financial independence.)

Obtain a Home Equity Loan (or Downsize the House) and Free Up Investment Capital

If you've owned a home for a number of years, you've built up tens (perhaps hundreds) of thousands of dollars of equity. Use either a home equity loan or a cash-out refinance to raise money at reasonable rates. Some homeowners refinance their homes with cash-out mortgages and use the proceeds for all cash bids on fix-up properties at discount prices.

> **A low-cost home equity loan makes an excellent source of cash to expand your real estate wealth.**

If your home has proven itself to be a good investment, leverage up. Use that equity to buy and renovate properties. Don't let cash sit idle when you could employ it to accelerate wealth building.

Bring in Partners

Do you know people who would like to earn the profits that real estate can provide but lack the time

> **Right now, millions of people with money would like to invest in real estate.**

or interest to take an active role? Investing partners can provide cash to the deal and enhance your credibility and borrowing power.

Although space here doesn't permit a full discussion of the legal, tax, and practical issues that partnerships can entail, I will urge you to look into this approach to raising cash for investment. I have brought in a partner on a number of my property purchases. All have worked out well for both me and the partner(s).

Attract Money with a Business Plan   Once you gain experience and credibility, you will raise money based on your reputation and achievements. When you're just getting started, write out a business plan for two reasons:

1. *Think it through.* Writing a plan forces you to think through your project from start to finish. As you write, you clarify. You see glitches (and perhaps opportunities) that more casual analysis frequently misses.

2. *Credibility.* Which of the following approaches would most likely persuade you to invest in a project? Someone asks, "Hey, how would you like to invest $20,000 in a rehab deal I'm putting together?" Or she says, "Here's a copy of my business plan for a rehab project that I'm doing. As you can see from this market and financial analysis, a $20,000 investment will pay you back $30,000 within six months."

> **Partners can provide the money. You provide the talent and time.**

To write this plan, highlight the market and property data discussed in earlier chapters as well as the expenditure, revenue, and profit calculations shown in Figure 3.1. To enhance credibility, pinpoint risk factors and how you are prepared to deal with them. For example,

◆ What if interest rates go up?
◆ What if renovation costs exceed the estimate?

<table>
<tr><td>

**Don't
overpromise.
Anticipate risks.**

</td><td>

♦ What if the renovations take longer than planned?
♦ What if sales (or rental) prices begin to soften?

</td></tr>
</table>

Entrepreneurs realize that no one perfectly predicts the future. You can, though, anticipate problems, and beforehand alleviate, reduce, or eliminate them. "What if _____ happens?" Build safeguards into your plans and prepare multiple exit strategies.

Favored Partners   Since even the most promising partnerships (aka marriages) can break down into contentiousness, choose someone who's reasonable, easy to get along with, and lives by a code of personal integrity and fairness. If plans go awry, as they sometimes do, you want a partner who will look at reasonable and fair ways to resolve the cause of the detour and cooperatively steer the project back on track.

**Choose a person
with character
first, money
second.**

Run from partners who insist that you sign a 10-page, fine-print partnership agreement that has been drafted by his or her lawyer. The more you let the lawyers intercede into your agreement, the more likely you and your partner will come to discord. Here I'm talking about small deals—not multimillion-dollar agreements when, like it or not, the lawyers often participate in the partnership negotiations.

Lawyers lead you to believe that a good partnership requires an "airtight" fine-print partnership agreement that precisely spells out each partner's rights and responsibilities. Not true! A good partnership requires good people as partners. If, for small deals, you (or your partner) think you need a 10-page document of legal jargon to set the terms of your agreement, that partnership is headed for trouble.

In your eagerness to do a deal, never reach for the money until you are confident that your investor will make a great partner. No contract ever substitutes for character.

Second Mortgages

You find a promising property, a motivated seller, and a low-interest rate assumable (or subject-to) mortgage. You face only one problem: The

> **Seller seconds reduce the amount of cash you need to close.**

existing mortgage shows a balance of $190,000, and the owner wants a price of $225,000. You can come up with only $20,000 in cash. How might you raise this $15,000? Use a second mortgage.

First, ask the seller to carry back a $15,000 lien against the property. If the seller won't or can't oblige you, turn to an institutional or private mortgage lender to provide the money. In the world of investment real estate (and in the world of homebuyers), cash-short buyers use second mortgages to close the gap between the amount of the primary financing and the purchase price of the property.

Cash Advances

You probably receive dozens of credit card offers every month. Some investors take advantage of these multiple offers and gain cash advance credit lines of $50,000, $100,000, or more. When they need quick money for a down payment, fix-up costs, or even total funding, they draw on their multiple cards for cash.

Should you pursue this method of financing? Maybe, but stick to these strict guidelines for borrowing and payback:

- *Bid limits.* Never use easy money to boost your bid limit for a property. Ready credit (either OWC or cash advances) can lure you into overpaying. Work the profit potential of the deal (see Figure 3.1). Then hold fast to your numbers. Excess credit causes many beginning investors to abandon their good sense.
- *Productive versus unproductive borrowing.* Worse than overpaying for a property, some would-be investors squander their credit lines on unproductive consumer spending (vacations,

clothes, jewelry, home decorating, entertainment). If you can't resist temptation, avoid multiple credit cards.

◆ *Rapid payback.* When you use cash advance credit lines for acquisition or renovation, pay the money back as soon as you generate profits through a property sale or refinance. Credit card borrowing not only eats away your profits, it reduces your ability to borrow mortgage money in the future.

◆ *FICO credit scores.* Even without borrowing, holding 6 to 10 credit cards with tens of thousands of dollars in available credit may pull down your credit scores. If such a tactic brings you down to a FICO of 740 from 780, that's no reason for concern. If multiple card applications drop your score from 628 to 575, avoid extending your credit lines through credit cards. (For more on credit scoring, see myfico.com and creditaccuracy.com.)

Cash advances can boost your ability to quickly place good deals under contract when they come your way. But, unwise (profligate) use of credit card debt ruins the fiscal fitness of many hopeful wealth builders. Avoid the risk unless you're confident that you can discipline both your borrowing and your payback.

Since the 1970s, various books and bootcamps have promoted "no cash, no credit, no problem" techniques for investors. True, many such promoters exaggerate the possibilities and understate the risks of their suggested deal making. Nevertheless, most investors I know who now enjoy net worths of seven figures (or more) started out with little or no cash. In real estate, knowledge of properties, knowledge of the market, and an entrepreneurial vision count far more than a big bank account or 760 FICO scores.

So, now it's up to you. Put the knowledge you've gained from this book into practice. You will create value for others—and you will build wealth for yourself. I wish you good fortune.

INDEX

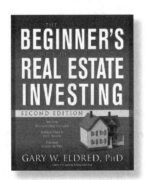

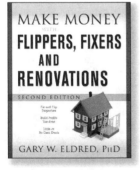

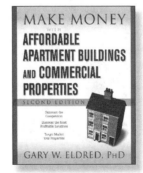